ንጉሠ ።

"NEGUS"
Majestic Tradition of Ethiopia

Miguel F. Brooks
Author of **Kebra Nagast** (The Glory of Kings)

LMH Publishing Limited

Cover Design by: Errol Rhule, Jamaica

Design & Typeset by: Michelle M.A. Mitchell, Jamaica

Published by: LMH Publishing Limited
7 Norman Road,
LOJ Industrial Complex,
Building 10,
Kingston C.S.O., Jamaica.
Tel: 876-938-0005; 938-0712
Fax: 876-928-8036
Email: lmhpublishing@cwjamaica.com

Printed by Lightning Source Inc., USA.   ISBN   976-8184-15-9

Dedication

To Our Grandparents,

Victims of the Great African Holocaust;

For they were made to endure the Hellish

Grindstone of Britannia' s Slave Enterprise.

We have not forgotten.. .We have not forgiven...

Acknowledgements

My profound gratitude and sincere thanks goes out, to the many persons and institutions who in one way or another have contributed towards the successful completion of this work. I especially recognize the abundance of research material, historical and biographical data, rare archival photographs, drawings and maps that were kindly provided, as well as the timely advice and suggestions offered.

Special thanks to Haile Mikael (Ethiopian World Federation), His Eminence Archbishop Abuna Yesehaq (Ethiopian Orthodox Church), Reginald Trelford and Arianne Giraud, Noel Pottinger (The Twelve Tribes of Israel), Bernard Jankee and Simone Lynch of the African Caribbean Institute of Jamaica, Paul Stewart of West Indies College Dept. of Information Sciences, Hazel Williams-Vaz, Kwame Tyndale, Johnette Simmons, Charmaine Stubbs, Ras Marshall Henry (The Imperial House), Ras Ivi Tafari and Ras Padaishaan of the International Nyahbinghi Order, Jamaica, and Atsede Mariam (E.O.C.).

Grateful thanks to my erudite and fearless publisher the Hon. Mr. Mike Henry, MP, who gave me invaluable guidance and constant support.

Finally, I wish to thank the numerous brethren, friends and associates, who gave me great encouragement and moral support in the face of daunting challenges and opposition. You were all a tower of strength and a source of fortitude and inspiration.

Contents

Preface

BOOK I
The Beginning...

Her throne was reputed to be an exquisitely crafted marvel of
solid gold richly ornamented with a profusion of precious
stones. Securely hidden in a secret cave and guarded by 300
fierce warriors, Makeda's throne seemed to be safe, yet King
Solomon's wisdom prevailed upon the exotic and enchanting
Queen of Sheba causing her to yield both throne and virtue,
unaware that she was so doing.

"Neither hammer nor ax nor any tool of iron was heard in the
Temple while it was in building" (I Kings 6:7) An astounding
narrative of the amazing miraculous means used by King
Solomon in the building of the Temple of God. In a dramatic
epic story spanning centuries from Eden to the Cross, and
from the Queen of Ethiopia to the traitor Judas, a startling

insight into the unerring fulfillment of many prophecies in the Old and New Testament is made evident, along with the devious cunning of Solomon, craftily spinning a web of deception around the beautiful black Queen and finally working his will on her.

"She came from the uttermost parts of the earth to hear of the wisdom of Solomon," yet he at once knew that she was lying, that her intent was other than her words, and so, he proceeded to teach the Queen of the South, lessons in wisdom and humility that she would never forget. Sourced from rare ancient manuscripts, this account will reveal hidden facets of the fascinating and ever-intriguing "greatest historical love-affair."

BOOK II
Unto our Days...

The Legendary, Biblical line of Solomonic kings of Ethiopia whose origins are enshrouded in the mists of remotest history, undoubtedly fulfill the divinely established Davidic Covenant. This Blessed Seed coursing through the sacred royal blood of 225 monarchs, survived the countless plots, intrigues and machinations of various enemies, to manifest the Kingly Character of the Anointed One in the exalted personality of the Elect of God, the Lion of the Tribe of Judah, Haile Selassie I. A powerful overview of the incredible trajectory through Bible, History and World-Affairs of the oldest Royal Dynasty in the annals of mankind.

One on the left, the other on the right beside the crucified
Lamb of God. But, were they really strangers to each other?
Or, had some rare quirk of destiny intertwine the lifepaths of
despicable thieves with that of the Saviour? This Biblical
drama of Ethiopian origins shows a hitherto unknown side to
the Gospel account of Iyesus' (Jesus') life, giving us a rare
glimpse into thought-provoking aspects of the doctrine of
predestination, the foreknowledge of God and the ultimate
destiny of man. Shocking and controversial, it's sure to
stimulate long and intense debate within Christendom and
beyond.

A harrowing account of the relentless transcultural journey of
a divinely selected people, carrying in their blood and genes
the legacy and compelling destiny of a special prophetic
mission. From ancient Nubia, Ethiopia, Egypt and across the
African continent to the great kingdoms of Ghana, Mali and
Songhai, the legendary Koromantyns of the Ashanti tribe
survived the hellish Middle Passage transportation across the
Atlantic, to lead every slave rebellion in Jamaica, and eventually to manifest the original spirit of Judah in the phenomena
of the Ras Tafarian movement. A first-time-ever history of the
spiritual origins of the Ras Tafarian people and the majestic
role they fulfill in last-day events. Riveting and controversial,
it will surely rock the comfortable assumptions of conven-
tional beliefs.

Preface

Steeped in impressive Biblical tradition, the origins of which are so remote that they are lost in the mists of antiquity and defy all efforts to trace their sources, Ethiopia, the incense country, the Divine Land, continues to mesmerize and enchant countless generations with the powerful imagery of its rich history and culture.

The exotic, the mysterious and the mystical, along with its millennial heritage and a vast and glorious history of cultural and intellectual sophistication, have made Ethiopia a frequent subject of research and study, both, in Ethiopia itself, and throughout the world.

This investigative activity into virtually all aspects of the life, culture and history of Ethiopia, has generated through the centuries a very substantial body of literature, in many languages, containing detailed accounts of events, reports of epic and historical import, religious and sacred literature, liturgical treasures, icons, art and numerous other facets of her daily life.

In its rich and oftentimes turbulent history spanning over two thousand years of its documented annals, Ethiopia has bequeathed the world a fascinating view into one of the most enigmatic and impressive empires known to mankind. Ethiopia's cultural legacy is undoubtedly one that will continue to be assiduously studied and revealed unto a world that is still searching for meaning and direction to the mystery of life.

In bringing forth this selection of six legends of Ethiopian origins, I have sought to offer a varied, though necessarily limited panoramic view, into the sources of her astounding and majestic trajectory through the unending flow of humanity's historical drama.

Amongst the many legends that make up the voluminous body of Ethiopian traditions, the Royal Epic of the Queen of Sheba, one of the most mysterious personalities in the Old Testament, is most likely the best known one in the Western World.

I have therefore, begun this selection of the Great Legends of Ethiopia, with three traditional narratives based on the Royal Chronicles of Abyssinia and other scholarly sources, which reveal many surprising and fascinating aspects of the enchanting and ever intriguing personality of the Queen of Sheba.

The second half of this sextet of legends are less familiar to Western readers, and will undoubtedly prove to be controversial and even disturbing to many, as I had, earlier on during the research stages of its compilation, decided not to suppress or withhold any of the factual aspects given in the sources consulted, nor to dilute the psycho-emotional impact of their contents.

The universal validity of Ethiopia's cultural legacy is made manifest in the enduring fascination and perennial interest that countless generations of Ethiopianists, Biblical scholars, historians and Africanist chroniclers, along with the general searcher into the vast treasure trove of her astounding heritage and traditions, have shown throughout the ages.

It is my fervent hope that this effort towards a further dissemination of Ethiopia's majestic legendary traditions, will stimulate additional research and publication from the vast quantum of her monumental literary history.

BOOK ONE

The Beginning...

CHAPTER 1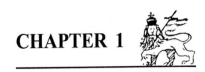

The Throne of Balkis

Her fame had already attained legendary proportions throughout most of the then known world. Storytellers and minstrels voiced the glories of her vast empire, the devastating power of her mighty armies and the wealth and dazzling pomp and pageantry that marked the royal court of Makeda, Queen of Sheba, monarch by divine right of the two Kingdoms, Ethiopia and Egypt.

In her unstoppable drive for even more dominion, she had conquered and subjugated numerous smaller nations, tribes and kingdoms, and had brought them firmly into the fold of her ever growing sphere of supreme authority.

But in the wider world, in far away lands beyond, it was the celebrated exquisite beauty of the virgin queen which never ceased to inspire countless songs, odes and poems to this magnificent and emigmatic ruler. For, she continually excited the keenest pleasures and emotional delight in all who had the good fortune to behold her.

And she now found herself pondering deeply about the future of her great kingdom, especially in respect of the royal succession, for, being childless and without a husband, the continuity of her dynasty was truly in doubt.

Nevertheless, she found some comfort in the fact that the stability of the royal realm was secure for the time being, as opulent riches constantly poured into the treasury's coffers, and her lucrative overland trade routes stretching from Western India, Persia and Arabia, unto North Africa, Syria and Palestine, received taxes and tribute from the many caravans that carried on the rich commerce of antiquity. Balkis, Queen of Sheba, was undoubtedly the most powerful and wealthiest woman of her days, ruler absolute of her enormous domain, which extended from Ethiopia in Africa unto India in Asia.

She was alone at the time, in her private quarters when a most shocking thing happened. Through an open window flew a strange bird, who after flying around her head, dropped a letter in her lap.

Startled at the rare event, she opened the letter and read:

"Greetings from Solomon, Son of David and servant of the Most High God, unto Balkis Queen of Sheba. You are aware that God has made me Lord and King over the wild beasts and the birds of heaven, also over the devils and spirits and ghosts of the night. You are aware moreover, that God has made me great Lord over all kings from the lands of the rising to the land of the setting sun.... Rise, therefore, not up against me, but come and surrender yourself unto me. Do as I bid and no harm, but much honour, will be yours.... But if you disobey my command and try to resist me, I shall send against you my armies of ghosts and devils which will slay you in your bed at night; and my armies of birds and wild beasts will tear your flesh and chew your bones..."

Her astonishment was great when she realized the import of the forceful contents of that imperious message from another monarch. But she had received many reports describing the wisdom, wealth and power of Solomon, King of Judah and Israel. Those glowing prescriptions had implanted stirrings in her mind and an intense curiosity about the great Jewish king, reputedly "the wisest man who ever lived."

Discretely and quietly she consulted her councillors and wise men, who promptly advised her to try to placate Solomon with gestures of friendship and goodwill, until they could find out the truth about his reputed wisdom and powers. Balkis then decided to send unto King Solomon an ambassador who would give to the king in Jerusalem a wide assortment of presents from her kingdom. These included five hundred bricks of gold, one thousand carpets woven of gold and silver thread, five hundred girls dressed as boys and five hundred boys dressed as girls, also a large crystal goblet which Solomon would be asked to fill with water which came "neither from heaven nor earth."

Balkis felt that if King Solomon was really filled with a divine wisdom, then it would not be difficult for him to distinguish the boys from the girls, despite their dress; neither would the filling of the goblet with mystical water be a problem for him.

Her councillors and her wise men agreed that if Solomon could accomplish these things, he was indeed a powerful wizard and it would be wise for the empire of Balkis Queen of Sheba to readily submit to him. The Queen however, wondered within her heart if perchance both realms could be united, thus making a new and greater kingdom while ensuring continuity of the royal succession.

At this time King Solomon was traveling in the region of Araby, moving swiftly from one city to another upon his mighty magic carpet made of green silk, which was so large that he and all of his armies as well as his great throne, were transported at the king's command through the air with lightening speed upon the wind. And Solomon discovered that the desert countries could not provide enough water for him, his harem and servants to take a bath, so he ordered his faithful lapwing - the strange bird which had delivered his letter to the Queen- to search out the whole country for a well.

So, in keeping with Solomon's command, the lapwing kept flying over the desert but found no source of water. Then it flew to the delightful land, the country of Eden, and there the lapwing sighted the city of the Queen with all its riches and abundant waters, also the beautiful Balkis, its beloved Queen. Upon returning to Solomon, the lapwing reported to the king all that she had seen. It was this glowing account that had inspired the mighty king to send his letter by the lapwing to Balkis, ordering her to surrender herself and her kingdom to him.

3

Meanwhile, the embassy that Balkis had sent with gifts unto King Solomon was all ready to set out on their mission, but were unable to depart as they did not know where to find the king. But Solomon, knowing that they were seeking him, had his 'Jinni' roll out the green magic carpet up to the very spot where the members of the embassy were standing and wondering which way to go. They unwittingly stepped on to the carpet and were astonished a short while after, to find themselves in the presence of King Solomon, as there he was arrayed in all his glory and seated upon his mighty throne. The embassy proceeded to present their wide assortment of gifts to the king, and when those presents that were intended to mystify him were presented to him, he quickly unravelled each one with no difficulty whatsoever.

And the ambassadors of Queen Balkis returned to their country and reported to their lady in detail all that had happened in their encounter with King Solomon. She then decided at once, in keeping with a promise she had made to herself, to go on the long journey to Jerusalem, to see this wonder-working monarch, as she was convinced that there was nothing she could do but to capitulate to the mighty King of Israel.

And so, preparations for the long and arduous trip from Ethiopia to the city of the king, Jerusalem, got under way. Twelve thousand chosen soldiers made up the personal guard of the Queen of Sheba, and there were also numerous servants, councillors, administrators, slaves and others who made up her vast retinue. Every beast of burden and every slave carried load according to his size and strength, for there was much equipment and merchandise and gifts to be carried on this most important royal mission.

King Solomon had received certain intelligence concerning the famed throne of Balkis, for his ambassadors and his spies had reported to him that her throne was an exquisitely crafted marvel of solid gold encrusted with a profusion of precious stones, giving forth multicoloured lights that bedazzled the eyes of all who came before it. And so, all these fabulous descriptions about the richly ornamented throne of Balkis, the beautiful black Queen of

Ethiopia, Queen of Sheba, served only to further intensify the eager curiosity that worked its grasp upon Solomon's mind. There was of course in the king's heart a touch of jealousy, envy perhaps, at the thought of a rival monarch seated on such a powerfully impressive throne.

For truly, that famous throne which was the symbol of her ancestral claim to rulership, she inherited along with the other royal signs of a divinely bestowed queenship; the scepter and the bandlet of righteousness, and the diadem upon the triple crown; all these came through the generations from ancient dynasties going back to the snake-worshipping Arwe Royal line. Of these, the "throne of Balkis" being the larger and more visible one, came to be the object of popular talk and speculation.

And so, when her captains and her master of caravans gave the order for all to rise and set out on the year-long journey to Jerusalem, Balkis had already secured her throne deep in the confines of a secret cave, and guarded by three hundred fierce warriors who were sworn to protect it with their lives unto the end.

Many months later, when the advance party of the great caravan of the Queen of the South, Balkis Queen of Sheba was sighted near Jerusalem, Solomon King of Israel and of Judah was holding audience and trying cases in the throne hall in the palace, as was his daily custom. Suddenly the King asked of his assembled mighty ones: "Which one of you can show me the throne of Balkis?" To which his chief Jinni responded that as soon as the king finished trying cases on this day, he would have the throne of Balkis before him. Then the impetuous young man, Asaph the grandson of the prophet Nathan, rose and said: "You cause the King to wait too long for this. Oh great King, before you can cast your eyes to heaven and back to earth, I shall have the throne of Balkis before you." Solomon looked up, and upon looking down again, there before his eyes was the fabulous throne of Balkis, brought forth by the mystical powers of the young wizard.

There it stood before their unbelieving eyes, in all its resplendent magnificence, the fabled throne of Balkis. From its high,

5

richly carved back and headrest, to it's four resting legs patterned as the paws of lions, the entire throne seat was profusely decorated with myriad, precious stones of varying sizes, each one reflecting at the same instant a phantasmagoric kaleidoscope of multicoloured lights, bewitching to the eyes in its live-like qualities.

It was the armrests however, that caught the attention of those assembled in Solomon's throne hall, for each had a huge stone embedded at the point where the queen's hand would rest. On the left armrest was a large ruby and on the right armrest was a diamond, both of the size and shape of a full-sized almond. And King Solomon summoned his master artisans, those skilled in working with gold, silver and all manner of gems and precious stones. He ordered them to transpose the two large gems that ornated each armrest; so, they changed the original position of each: the ruby going to the right armrest and the diamond being placed upon the left armrest where the ruby had been. Then the throne of Balkis was placed in one of the treasure rooms in Solomon's palace.

When at length the royal visitor arrived amidst all the exotic panoply and regal magnificence of her portable court, she was received by King Solomon and the nobles of Jerusalem with all the high honours that such an exalted monarch is due. And the people hailed her repeatedly: Long live Balkis, Queen of Sheba! Then Solomon decided to confront the queen with a surprising and rare question. He said unto her: "The magnificence of your fabled throne has traveled ahead of thee, surely to remain here with us if your exquisite majesty forever abides in this land. But do come with me and behold once more the throne of your royalty."

Balkis said not a word, but allowed King Solomon to guide her to the treasure room of the palace, and there she saw the throne, the seat of her majesty and rulership. Her astonishment gave way to puzzled amazement as her eyes remained fastened to the beautiful throne seat that stood before her. And Balkis wondered immediately about the throne she had left securely guarded in the depths of the cave of her Ethiopian mountain realm. But then, how could it have reached Jerusalem ahead of her? It all seemed so unreal.

And as she pondered upon these possibilities, she noticed something that made her smile, and looking at Solomon she said: "From being a wise man thou hast turned thyself into a lowly trickster. This furniture which is made manifest to me, is but a clever copy of my throne, yet the armrest stones are not properly placed, thus I know that this is not my true royal throne. Thou mayest keep it and so be reminded of the magnificence and greatness of my kingdom."

To which King Solomon replied: "Thou speakest truthfully, for thy kingdom is great and mighty even without the fabled throne of Balkis. The Lord and God of the universe has chosen thee and hast made thee a blessed woman, and greater blessings shall come unto thee because thou hast journeyed from the uttermost parts of the earth to learn about the Creator and his wonderful works."

And so Solomon made Balkis, Queen of Sheba, his wife and converted her from sunworship to the worship of the one true God. She had given the whole of her realm to Solomon but he returned it to her. And when at length she returned to her own kingdom she carried within her the fruit of her union with Solomon, and after that, she brought forth a man-child who subsequently became the ancestor of the Ethiopian kings.

But the legendary throne of Balkis returned not with the queen to Ethiopia, but remained with Solomon the King in Jerusalem. And the three hundred chosen soldiers who were guarding the throne of Balkis deep in the bowels of the earth, were burned alive in their own clothes along with their families and their homes.

And so ends the chronicle of the throne of Balkis.

CHAPTER 2

"The Temple of God and the Wood of the Cross"

In those days after the death of his father David, the son of Jesse, who had reigned over the children of Israel, King Solomon in accordance with his most excellent wish began to build the house of God in Jerusalem. And this was the desire of the Almighty, for He had said unto David that although David was a man after His own heart, nevertheless his hands were too steeped in blood, and therefore it would be that son from his union with Bathsheba, the almond-eyed beauty whom he had taken from his General Uriah through a despicable plan of deceit, whom He desired to build a house unto the Lord.

And David had begun to accumulate and store up vast quantities of all manner of materials, for the building of the great temple of God. Precious wood from Lebanon, from Syria and Persia; stone and marble from distant quarries in Palmyra, Bozrah and the land of Padan Aram. And the plan of the temple was revealed to King Solomon by means of a vision that God had sent unto him, for the shape of the temple and its ground plan, the angle and the lines of the same, and its columns and its arches, were all conveying to the initiated ones, in symbol and in measurements, the secret of God's Master Plan of Creation and the perfections of His ineffable powers.

In accordance to the Divine Plan, Solomon the King gave the command for the stones to be hewn in immense sizes, as the building was to be a great and magnificent one, reflecting the rays of the sun and shining resplendent for all to see even from great distances of that city of God, Jerusalem. But the workmen were unable to hew such large blocks of stone, and their tools broke when they attempted the work, and so they cried out to Solomon the King and besought him to ponder and think out in his wisdom some way for them to accomplish their labour. And Solomon entreated God, the Supreme bestower of wisdom, to suggest some means to him by which the huge stones could be cut.

And behold, all the workmen, the courtiers, counsellors and noblemen gathered together along with King Solomon in the courtyard of the royal palace. Then Solomon summoned the hunters and commanded them to bring forth a young Rukh bird from its nest, and in accordance with the orders they brought a young Rukh bird from its nest. And he commanded them likewise to bring a large brass pot with a space inside it sufficient to contain the Rukh bird. The pot had three legs, each one a cubit in height, and it stood upon the ground. Then Solomon commanded them to set down the Rukh bird spreadeagled in the palace courtyard and to put the brass pot over it, and the wings and the head of the bird protruded from under the pot, and raised it above the ground.

When the mother Rukh bird returned to her nest in the high mountains and did not find her young one there, she was greatly disturbed, and she flew round and round tirelessly over the earth seeking for her young one. Then she flew over Jerusalem and saw her young one under the pot, but was powerless to seize it from under the brass pot. And she flew away into the heights and went towards the Paradise of God, the Garden of Delight, which is within the land of Ethiopia of old, and there in the eastern part of Eden, she found a piece of wood which had been cast down there as if for her to carry it away. And so the mother Rukh bird seized the piece of wood, and by reason of her great sorrow for her young one she took no rest until she had brought it to Jerusalem, and she hurled it down upon the brass pot.

And then, by the might of God, a miracle took place forthwith, for the pot instantly split into two halves, and the mother Rukh saw her young one and caught it up and took it away to her

9

nest. So, when King Solomon and his nobles, courtiers, counsellors and all the workmen saw this miracle, with a loud voice they praised the Almighty, who had bestowed a bird that was not endowed with reasoning powers, the ability to do such a thing which human beings could not do.

Immediately King Solomon ordered the stonemasons to take that piece of holy and blessed wood, so that, after they had marked out and measured the stone which they wished to split, they needed only to lay the piece of wood on the place marked upon the stone. And when they had done this, by the might and power of God the stone split wherever they wished it to split, and so the workmen found their work easy. King Solomon himself became certain in his mind that the Governor of the Universe regarded the building of the Holy Temple with favour.

When the construction of the temple was finished, that piece of wood, which was found to be alive and growing though no water came near to it, remained in the entrance chamber of the forecourt of the porch. As the building of the temple had ceased, the operative power of the piece of wood came to an end, and with the passing of time many no longer remembered the wonders that it had wrought.

But God had decided that the kingdom of David and his son Solomon should be transferred to the blessed land of Abyssinia-Ethiopia and so he stirred up in the heart of the Queen of that country an intense desire to make a journey to Jerusalem to "hear the wisdom of Solomon" as the scriptures say.

And behold, from the earliest times the kingdom of Abyssinia was ruled by ancient dynasties whose domains extended far beyond the present-day geographic boundaries of modern Ethiopia; for in the days of its greatest extent the kingdom encompassed the entire Nile river valley and lowlands including Nubia, present day Sudan and Egypt towards the north, and across the Red sea unto the Arabian peninsula, Persia and India in the East.

The dynasty to which Makeda belonged is estimated to have been established in Ethiopia around the year 1300 BC and was founded by Za Besi Angabo who replaced the last representative of an older Ethiopian dynasty, the Arwe royal line. The dynasty inaugurated by Za Besi Angabo ruled over the nation for about 350 years, and the last two of its monarchs were Queen Makeda's grandfather and father respectively. Her grandfather was Za Sebado who reigned from about 1076-1026 B.C.; his wife and queen was named Ceres. They had an only child, a daughter, who married Za Sebado's chief minister. When Za Sebado died this son-in-law became the country's king, and reigned from about 1026-1005 B.C. To him and his wife Queen Ismenie, were born two children; first a son, Prince Noural Rouz, whose name meant "the light of day"; and second, a daughter, Princess Makeda, who is said to have been born in 1020 B.C. While Prince Noural was still an infant his nurse accidentally let him fall into the fire which caused his death.

When her father died in about the year 1005 B.C., Makeda, being his only heir, ascended the throne and reigned until about the year 955 B.C. The young queen is said to have been very beautiful in face, her stature was absolutely superb and her understanding and intelligence were very great. And in the Ethiopian Royal Chronicles it is further reported that she was exceedingly rich, for God had given her glory and wealth and gold and silver, splendid apparel and camels and slaves and caravans which traded for her by sea and by land from India unto Syene (within modern day Egypt).

And when the mother of the Queen of Sheba, Queen Ismenie, was with child of her, she saw a fat goat, and she looked upon it with greedy desire, and she said, "How attractive it is! And how fat and handsome it's feet are!" And she longed for it, wanting to eat of its flesh in the manner of women who are with child. But she ate not of the goat. And when the daughter was fashioned completely in the womb of her mother, she had one foot like the foot of human beings and the other like the foot of a goat.

So then, the mother of the Queen brought forth this extraordinary being, and loved her and raised her in motherly love, but when the maiden was ready for marriage, she did not want to

11

marry any man because of her malformed and profusely hairy foot; so she continued in her virginity until she began to reign. And then the thought to visit Solomon, the reputed "wisest man who ever lived" arose in her mind with such great intensity and bewildering fascination, as was ordained in the wisdom of God, for the Almighty had decided that the kingdom of David should last even unto the end of the world.

And truly, God hath said in his word: "The Lord hath sworn in truth unto David; He will not turn from it; of the fruit of thy body will I set upon thy throne. If thy children shall keep my covenant and my testimony that I shall teach them, their children will also sit upon thy throne for evermore."[1]

And the Children of Israel did change the covenant, and did not observe the truth, and rejected Him who was expected, therefore the kingdom was to be taken away from them, so God rent from them Prophecy, Priesthood and Sovereignty.

Solomon the King had heard of the imminent arrival of the exotic monarch from the great kingdom of the southern regions, the Queen of Sheba, Queen of Ethiopia; and he was also informed of the magnificence of the immense caravan that made up her royal entourage, with the perfumed horses, the hundreds of camels, asses, mules, soldiers, slaves and sundry attendants, all loaded with provisions, wares and merchandise, and also vast quantities of the precious things of her realm:

Aromatic gums, incense, cassia, myrrh, spices, gold, emeralds; As for precious stones, her gifts to King Solomon also included harvests of pearls from Ethiopia's Red Sea isles, sapphires, and the famous Topazes of Ethiopia. The ancient world was well aware of the vast wealth of the "blessed land of Punt" the traditional Egyptian designation for Queen Makeda's ancestral domain, and her kingdom had been famous for the varieties and abundance of its spice plants, its ebony, ivory and apes. All these and much more made up the Queen of Sheba's reported gifts to King Solomon.

---

[1] *Psalm 132:11,12*

When the Queen arrived on the outskirts of Jerusalem, the dazzling sight of the resplendent Temple of God reflecting the sunlight from its dome and marble walls high upon temple mount, filled her heart with a strange foreboding and great bewilderment at the majestic sight that gradually unfolded to her eyes. The pomp and exuberant ritual and ceremony that attended her royal carriage, with all the luxurious and richly ornamented retinue, were a fitting encounter in her glorious entrance to the magnificent City of God, Jerusalem.

Solomon the King had been well informed by his ambassadors and spies on many matters pertaining to the great visiting monarch, and was quite certain from the information which he had received, that one of her feet was as the foot of a goat. He therefore planned a cunning plan in his wisdom whereby he might be able to see her foot without asking her to show it to him.

So then, Solomon the King placed his throne out at the side of the courtyard of the temple where he would have a vantage position and would be able to see the Queen approaching; then he ordered his servants to open up the floodgates of the irrigation channels so that the courtyard of the temple might be covered with water. This was done, and the piece of wood that was in the courtyard, having been brought there by the bird from Paradise, was submerged by the water, but no one noticed this which had been decreed by the wisdom of God.

When, at last, the Queen arrived at the gate of the temple and found the grounds covered by the water, she was determined to ride into the presence of King Solomon on her beast, but they made her to know that this was the entrance to the House of God, and being hallowed ground, no one might enter it riding on a beast. Reluctantly, Queen Makeda dismounted; at the same time deciding in her mind that a mere body of shallow water would not prevent her from coming into the presence of King Solomon. And as her servants supported her, she instinctively drew up the lower parts of her garments so that she might step into the water.

So it was that Solomon saw her feet without asking her to

show them to him. And behold, she stepped into the water in the courtyard slowly walking towards the King who was seated upon his throne a short distance away, when the foot that was fashioned like the foot of a goat touched the wood. Immediately the might of God made itself manifest, and the goat's foot became exactly like her other foot which was human. At once she understood that Divine Power that had seized her and a great fear and trembling came upon her, but she rejoiced within her heart and stepped further into the water and at length she came into the presence of King Solomon, who welcomed her with gladness and brought her up on his throne, and paid her honour, and permitted her to sit by his side.

And as the two monarchs sat side by side upon King Solomon's throne, all the nobles of the city of Jerusalem and all the people who were gathered there rejoiced and gave out great shouts of joy, and they all hailed and saluted the magnificent royalty of the two kingdoms, Jerusalem and Ethiopia.

And the Queen informed him that she had come from the ends of the earth solely to worship in Jerusalem and to hear his wisdom. Then she said to him: "When I came to thy honourable kingdom and dipped my foot into the water, that foot which was like the foot of a goat touched something that was submerged in the water and became at once like my other foot. Great fear and trembling came upon me, then joy, because of that which had happened to me through the compassion of the Governor of the Universe." And then she showed him both her feet. Then Solomon praised and glorified God, who alone worketh great and wonderful things, and makes manifest His boundless mercy, both, unto the mighty and unto the lowly.

Solomon then revealed to the Queen that it was he himself who had ordered the water to cover the courtyard, in order to cause her to lift her garments so that he might see her goat's foot. He then commanded the workers to make the waters go back to their place, and the ground of the courtyard became visible, and the piece of wood which she had touched with her feet stood out clearly.

Then Solomon related to her the story of the piece of wood, of how it had been brought to Jerusalem by the bird which had taken it from her dominions, from the Garden of Delight where the Tree of Life was, and how it had been used to split the massive blocks of stone to build the Temple of God, without the use of hammer or chisel or any iron instrument. It was truly a wood that signifieth life, and it was holy and blessed.

Makeda, Queen of Sheba, listened in wonderful amazement as Solomon narrated to her the mighty operations of the wood of life. And when the Queen understood all these things she commanded that honour should be paid to that piece of wood, and so she proceeded to decorate it with her Royal wristband of silver, the Bandlet of Righteousness that was used as a sign of rulership commonly called "Piece of Silver"; and when Solomon saw her do that, he also decorated the piece of wood with his royal silver wristband, and he designated a place of honour for the living wood of Paradise within the Temple of God. And it came to pass that each and every one of Solomon's successors, who came to the Temple of God to pray, as soon as they heard the story of the sacred piece of wood, decorated it also with their silver bandlet of rulership. And from the days of Solomon the King, to the coming of Christ, that piece of wood was decorated with thirty bandlets of silver.

Centuries later, when in the fullness of time, He whom God had sent, wished to complete His dispensation and to accomplish the deliverance of Adam and his posterity from out of the hand of the accursed enemy, Satan; the traitor Judas made a covenant with the high priests to deliver the Christ unto them, so that they might be able to condemn him to death. And so, the high priests undertook to give Judas the thirty bandlets of silver on the wood that was in the temple; and they had the piece of wood brought by night to the place where the high priests were, and they stripped from it, the thirty bandlets of silver, and delivered them over to Judas who took them, and in turn he delivered Christ by betrayal to the priests.

When the morning of the fifth day of the week had come, on

15

which they condemned the Lord Christ to death on the cross, being certain now that their evil intent was about to be fulfilled, they took that same holy and sacred wood, commanded a carpenter to make a cross out of it, and they crucified the Redeemer upon it.

Adam was led astray when he ate of the fruit of that tree in Paradise, and it was because of this that he was stripped of his glory and driven out from Paradise, and Satan reigned over him and over his race. Adam's deliverance took place by the dispensation of God with this piece of wood from the region of Paradise, and it became an honoured thing to kings, and at length the King of Kings came and was crucified upon it. And so, He the Christ, redeemed Adam and his descendants from the power of the Accursed one by means of a piece of wood from the tree of life, even as the fruit of that wood had led him into error. As for the thirty bandlets of silver, a veritable king's ransom that was given to Judas, he cast them back to the Pharisees, then he hanged himself and departed this life by reason of his inordinate love of money.

Thus, by means of that sacred and sanctified wood from Paradise, was accomplished both, the building of the Temple of God, and the redemption of mankind by the sacrificial death of the Second Adam, Christ.

CHAPTER 3

The Lying Queen

*"And when the Queen of Sheba heard of the fame of Solomon,
she came to prove Solomon with hard questions at Jerusalem..."*

II Chronicles 9:1

The beginnings of her ancient realm can no longer be truly known by modern man, for many are the traditions that claim a place in the annals and the chronicles of her millennarian kingdom. And even these are derived from traditions and practices that are considerably older, with numerous variants and changing versions.

One of the most popular versions tells how in the beginning the country worshipped a serpent to which an annual offering was made of a virgin bound to a tree. This serpent, called 'Arwe', was the first king, who ruled until the arrival of a mysterious stranger known as 'Angabo' who killed the serpent and rescued the maiden who was about to be sacrificed, married her, and obtained the throne. That virgin who was thus delivered from her fate was none other than Makeda or Balkis as she is known among the Arabs, and who became the Queen of Sheba, Queen of the South, the Queen of Ethiopia.

And her kingdom of Sheba was the home of the Sabaeans who used to trade in precious metals, jewels, spices and odoriferous resins; they had formed themselves into tribal confederacies that were governed by queens during the period of the ninth to seventh centuries B.C. Earlier, in about 1000 B.C., the Sabaeans had crossed the Red Sea and conquered the Hamites of Ethiopia, thus extending their kingdom to the African mainland, and by the first century A.D. the victors had established the kingdom of Aksum which was ruled by the Solomonic dynasty.

The Sabaeans had domesticated the camel in earlier times, and this had greatly increased their dominance over the old Arabian Incense Road, the traditional caravan route over which they moved vast quantities of incense, spices, gold and precious stones.

Makeda was a shrewd ruler who understood clearly the importance of maintaining control of the lucrative trade that moved from her domains, unto Egypt, Phoenicia, Palestine and Syria. She realized that her country's merchant camel caravans should be able to pass through the kingdom of Judah and Israel without being excessively taxed. So, she considered carefully and determined in her astute mind, that the need to strike trade agreements with Solomon King of Judah and Israel, would be the paramount consideration in her impending journey to Jerusalem.

And although Makeda continued to receive extensive reports pertaining to the land of Israel and its celebrated king, her curiosity about this wise, wonder-working potentate, and the many amazing judgments of righteousness that he made in difficult and seemingly unsolvable cases, caused her to ponder and to truly doubt the veracity of the reports. So, quietly she began to search out the means by which she could test the limits of Solomon's reputed wisdom. And she consulted with the wise men in her realm, those who could devise the most difficult problems which no one could resolve, for she found it hard to believe that there arose in the land of Israel a King who possessed wisdom so perfect and so great.

Makeda herself was a lover of wisdom, and God had given her a good measure of wise discernment by which she governed the affairs of her kingdom. But she and all her subjects were worshippers of the chief dieties of the heavenly triad, the Sun,

Moon, and Venus, to which temples and altars were dedicated as well as sacred enclosures wherein incense was burnt upon finely carved offering-stands. The temples were ornated with statues wrought in gold, silver and bronze, and in those days, a victory at war was always the occasion for the blood-sacrifice of both beasts and prisoners alike.

Yet, in spite of the inevitable acculturation that such primitive cultic practices would leave in the mind of the Queen, she nevertheless felt the tug of a higher call, bidding her to follow the subtle stirrings of her heart over the coarser paths of mundane reasonings. For, these inexplicable urgings were persistently saying to the exotically beautiful Sabaean-Ethiopian monarch, that a greater destiny and fulfillment awaits her in Jerusalem, the sacred city of the God-anointed king. And Solomon was said to be the wisest king in the world.

He was the king of Israel, and in those days people of all lands heard of his great wisdom, and they came from many countries to see this great king and to hear his righteous judgments and the perfect administration of his kingdom. And King Solomon was truly a man of God; for he was very loving and kind to all living beings. He even spoke the language of all animals. The creatures of the heavens and the beasts of the earth came to Solomon to converse with him and he understood the speech of the birds as they spoke to him, and they told Solomon of all things that they saw in far and distant lands, and so he came to know the things that happened in those other lands.

And so it was even between King Solomon and Hiram the King of Tyre, who was then known by birth of the tribe of Naphtali, on the mother's side, for she was of that tribe; but his father was Ur, of the stock of the Israelites. They constantly exchanged wise words and riddles and problems of great complexity, in friendly testing of each one's ability to solve the many dilemmas posed. And Hiram also was a great seeker after wisdom, and he gave unto Solomon great stores of the precious lumber of his country, and silver, and gold and many skilled craftsmen who worked on metal, on stone and on wood. And Hiram helped Solomon in the building of the Temple of God, but he doubted that King Solomon was the wisest king in the world.

And they both were at this time reclining and at ease in the palace, the house of King Solomon. And Hiram said unto Solomon:

"May the king live forever. Tell me Oh Great King; Which is the creature upon the face of the earth, that in the morning of its life, walks upon four limbs, in the midday of its life walks upon two limbs, and in the evening of its life walks upon three limbs?"

Then Solomon answered and said unto Hiram: "Is it not man, who as a babe crawleth upon four limbs, as an adult walketh upon two limbs, and as an aged man with a walking cane walketh upon three limbs? And there is no other creature upon the earth that changes the manner of his walking in this fashion, for God hath made man to be not as the beasts or the flying birds, but to be as unto Him."

So, Hiram King of Tyre marveled at the swiftness of King Solomon's answer and at the wisdom of his utterance, all of which he gave forth with the greatest ease and in sweetness of spirit, with a soft and musical voice which was like balm to the ears and like water to the thirsty man.

They both then heard commotion and noise within the palace, and they looked up and saw some of the king's servants pursuing a bee that had flown into the king's quarters. And the king's servants were angry with the bee and tried to kill it. They ran up and down the palace trying to catch the bee. And when Solomon saw his men running after the bee, he felt very sorry for it, and he did not want to see it killed, so, he stopped his men from killing it and he went and opened his window and let the little bee fly through it into freedom.

And Hiram King of Tyre noted the deep compassion that King

Solomon had, even for such a small creature as the bee, and he vowed within his heart to maintain a loyal friendship towards Solomon.

And the sagacity and wisdom which God had bestowed upon Solomon was so great, that he exceeded even the ancients, and in respect of the Egyptians, who are said to have been beyond all men in learning and understanding, he was in no way inferior to them, and indeed, it is evident that their acumen and sagacity was very much inferior to that of the king.

For Solomon also excelled and distinguished himself in wisdom among those who were most eminent among the Hebrews in those days for shrewdness. He also composed one thousand and five books of odes and songs, and three thousand books of parables and similitudes; for he used to speak a parable for every sort of tree from the hyssop to the cedar; and in like manner he also composed parables and philosophical discourses about the beasts, and about all sorts of living creatures, whether upon the earth, or in the seas, or in the heavens, as he was well acquainted with their natures and frequently demonstrated his exquisite knowledge about their several properties and virtues.

God had also given Solomon the ability to learn that skill which expels demons, and he had written numerous treatises on that science containing many incantations and the manner of using exorcisms, by which they drive away demons, so that they never return.

And so it is known that even centuries after, Eleazar the Jew, demonstrated in the presence of Vespasian and a multitude of his soldiers, and captains and the common people, how he could release men that were possessed by demons according to the procedure set by King Solomon in his treatises. And so, Eleazar would place a circle of the root of a Eleazarba plant mentioned by Solomon to the nostrils of the demoniac, after which he drew out the demon through the nostrils; and when the man fell down immediately after, he rebuked the demon that he should return into him no more. Eleazar then proceeded to demonstrate to the assembled multitude that the demon had in effect departed from the man, he set a basin full of water nearby and commanded the demon to overturn it, and when this was done forthwith, the skill and wisdom of Solomon was manifestly shown, that all may know the vastness of Solomon's abilities and the extraordinary virtues of every kind with which the king was endowed, and how he was beloved by God.

And even after Hiram the king of Tyre had departed to his own country, he continued to send many sophisms, riddles and enigmatical sayings to Solomon the king, desiring that he would solve them. But so sagacious and wise was Solomon, that none of these problems were too hard for him to solve, nor was their hidden meaning concealed from him.

Not only was Solomon celebrated and famous for his knowledge and extensive wisdom, but God had favoured him with immense wealth to which was added a good mind towards making excellent use of it. And the weight of gold that was annually brought to the king was six hundred and sixty-six talents (about sixty thousand pounds in weight); not including what was brought by the merchants nor the tribute that many kings of surrounding neighbouring nations sent to him. And all the great fame about him was voiced abroad, proclaiming the virtue and wisdom of Solomon, so that all the kings 'in every land were desirous to see him, as they did not believe what was reported, on account of its being almost incredible. Yet they also demonstrated the regard they had for him by the presents they made to him; for they sent him vessels of gold and silver, purple garments, many sorts of spices, horses, chariots, and numerous mules for his carriages. And these merely augmented those that he had before which were numbered in the thousands, for which fine stables were appointed. The riders of the horses were a further ornament upon them, for they were youths in the most delightful flower of their manhood, and they were clothed in beautiful garments all of Tyrian purple.

And so it was at that time that the reigning monarch of the two lands, Candace Queen of Egypt and Ethiopia, known also as

Makeda Queen of Sheba entered the dominions of Solomon King of Judah and Israel. For she was a true lover of wisdom, a woman as is rarely seen, inquisitive into philosophy, a strong and mighty ruler, who was also renowned for her extraordinary beauty and strong will. And when she heard of the virtue and prudence of Solomon, she had a great mind to see him, she being desirous to be satisfied by her own experience, to have a trial of his wisdom and to propose questions of great difficulty, and to determine if he could solve their hidden meaning.

As Solomon and Hiram were comfortably exchanging pleasantries in the throne hall, their easy conversation was suddenly interrupted by the blast of royal trumpets announcing the arrival of the long-expected queen. And they all looked out through the windows of the palace unto the causeway of black stone that was the main road that led to the royal city of Jerusalem, and that showed to many travelers and pilgrims in those days, the grandeur and the riches of the kingdom. And Solomon saw a great line of people coming to his palace amidst great excitement, and indeed, it was the rich and beautiful Ethiopian queen, the Queen of Sheba with many of her people. She had come with many gifts for the king.

Accordingly, she came to Jerusalem with great splendour and rich furniture; for she brought with her camels laden with gold, sweet spices and with precious stones, also many lions, monkeys and rare birds. She wanted to find out if Solomon was really the wisest man in the world.

The king then sent his men to bring the Queen of Sheba and her people to the palace. King Solomon sat upon his great throne with a lion on each side of the throne. These lions were very special, as they would roar if anyone did not tell the king the truth.

When the Queen of Sheba entered the palace she was surprised at the fineness and largeness of his royal palace, and the exuberant luxury and beauty of the apartments; and she was es-

23

pecially amazed and astonished beyond measure at the house which was called the *Forest of Lebanon*, and the apparel of the numerous servants, and everything about King Solomon's palace impressed her greatly for it was well made and beautiful.

As she approached Solomon with a few of her chosen attendants, their eyes met, and she noted that his were not the imperious eyes of one who is accustomed to wielding power and issuing commands, but rather, a quiet humility and calmness of disposition were in them; and it made her also to feel a sense of peace and quietude in her innermost self. "May the king live forever" said the queen. "I have come to learn of your great wisdom, Oh great king."

Suddenly, the lions began to roar, but the queen did not know why. It was because she had not spoken the truth. She had come to test the king to see if he was really the wisest man in the world. She did not believe all she had heard, and even while she stayed at the palace, she thought of many ways to show that Solomon was not as wise a man as people said. But every time she asked something Solomon would give her the right answer.

So it was, that one day the queen held a great banquet in honour of King Solomon, which was attended by a great many people. And the minstrels, the acrobats, the dancing girls, and the trained monkeys and the snake charmers were all entertaining the royal guests. Thus it was then, that the sumptuous meal with numerous courses of all manner of dainty meats, exotic fruits and the choicest wines were laid out in circumstances of the most skilful management and preparation.

At the end of the great dinner the queen spoke to King Solomon, and said: "The people say that you are the wisest man in the world. I have something to ask you. Can you tell me the right answer?" "I can try," replied the king in a calm and melodious voice. "What is it?"

The queen then sent her servants for six little children. They were all eleven years old and they all looked exactly the same, identical to each other. All of them had on the same clothes and their hair and their faces all looked the same.

"I have before you six children," said the queen. Of the six, three are girls, and three are boys. Can you tell which of them are girls, and which are boys without hearing them speak?"

For a long moment after, the great banquet hall remained quiet. Everyone was amazed at the perfect similarity in the appearance of the six children, for it was truly impossible to tell anyone of them apart from the others, such were their identical appearance and demeanor. This was something that everyone felt that Solomon could not answer. And the king himself was silent while he looked at the children intently and with a discerning gaze.

King Solomon then quietly asked God for wisdom and understanding to solve this dilemma posed by his royal visitor. All the people who were there assembled, were looking at him. After a short moment Solomon smiled. He then commanded his servants to bring some water, soap and a towel. After these were brought to the hall, he told them to bring a bucket of mud.

The king then turned to the children and told them to come forward. They at first timidly approached him, but he quickly put them at ease with his calm and pleasant manner and the sweet tone of his soothing voice. Solomon told the children to take some of the mud out of the bucket and play with it. After they had thus played with the mud for a while, he told them to wash their hands in the clean water and to dry them with the clean towel.

Everyone was looking at the strange ritual that was being played out by the children, as they obediently followed the king's instructions. And as they washed their hands and dried them, Solomon watched the children closely. Then he walked over to them.

"These three are boys, and these three are girls," said the king.

"You are right!" shouted the queen in surprise and disbelief. "How did you find out?"

King Solomon smiled. "Look at these three girls," he said. "They have washed their hands over and over again, very carefully. They took their time and washed their hands properly." Then Solomon showed her the three boys. "Look at their hands," he said. "They did not take the time to wash them properly. Little boys do not like to wash," said Solomon, while he gave the queen an enigmatic smile, for he knew all along that the queen was testing his wisdom and his skill in solving difficult problems as the one she had just presented to him.

Everyone was surprised to see that Solomon had found the right answer. He showed the people that indeed he was the wisest man in the world, but, the Queen of Sheba was still not convinced, and she determined to further test the king. Therefore she commanded the skilful artisans and craftsmen that were among her people, that they should make some flowers, and that the flowers that they would make should look exactly like the natural flowers that were in the garden of the king. She was sure that Solomon could never tell the living flowers from the man-made ones, for her artisans were extremely skillful and clever in the making of all manner of artificial ornaments that were identical to their natural models.

So, on this other occasion, the queen held another great dinner for King Solomon, and this time even more people came. And the queen told Solomon that she had a special gift for him. She then presented him with the flowers that her men had made. "My men are so great that they have made flowers just like the living ones in your garden," said the queen. "But one of these flowers that you see is not manmade. It is really from your garden. Can you tell me which one it is?"

At first Solomon felt that it would be easy to find the natural flower from the garden. But as he walked through the flowers, he discovered that they all really looked exactly the same.

The king stood there before the flowers for a long time unable to see any difference among them. And the guests noticed this, that the king appeared to be baffled by the seeming impossibility of telling the natural flower from the man-made ones. The people began to speak softly to each other, and the queen began to smile. They all felt that at last, this was something that Solomon could not answer.

Once again Solomon quietly asked God for wisdom and understanding. Then suddenly, Solomon felt something on his hand. It was the same bee he had saved from being killed. The little bee then flew off his hand and into the air, as Solomon watched it discretely, but none of the other people saw it. The bee flew over the flowers until it stopped on one of them. Then the bee went into the flower that had honey in it, and so, Solomon knew which flower was the living one. So he went and picked out the flower which came from his garden, turned to the smiling queen, and said, "Here is the flower that came from my garden."

The queen closely examined the flower. "It is really the flower from your garden," she said in a subdued voice. "I did not expect that you could ever find it." The people were surprised, and cheered the king for his great wisdom.

So she openly admitted that she was greatly amazed at the wisdom of Solomon, as she had discovered that it was more excellent upon trial than what she had heard by report beforehand; and she thanked the king for his kind reception of her, and the great desire to please her that he had shown. And she was not able to contain the surprise she was in, but confessed to him that, "I, indeed, who did not believe what was reported, am now in the greatest admiration imagined, for thy wisdom and thy grandeur are beyond expectation, for one would therefore bless God, who hath so loved this country and those that inhabit it, as to make thee king over them."

And as the Queen of Sheba had demonstrated by words the great admiration she had for Solomon the King, she also made her disposition known by the abundance of presents she gave him. Solomon also repaid her with many good things, principally by bestowing upon her what she chose of her own inclination, for there was nothing that she desired which he denied her; and he was very generous and liberal in his own heart, he showed the greatness of his soul in giving her whatever she herself desired of him.

And so at last, the Queen of Sheba believed that King Solomon was the wisest man in the world. "Your wisdom is even more than I heard," she said.

But King Solomon had also learned something special. From the bee, he learned that there was none so great that he did not need help, and there was none so small that he could not give help. And he also learned from the bee, that even the smallest of God's creatures are teachers of kings.

BOOK TWO

Unto Our Days...

CHAPTER 4

Dynasty of the Blessed Seed

The fascinating and almost mythical historical drama of the divinely established Solomonic dynasty of Kings of Ethiopia, has its prelude in the remotest annals of known history, a trail that takes us into the dry dusty books of the ancients where the path is widened and truth is revealed. Like a modern "Quest for the Holy Grail", this search for a long forgotten and much suppressed account leads us backward into the heart of the most precious primal roots from which all culture sprang.

When Herodotus spoke of old Ethiopia as the land where "the Gods delighted to banquet with the pious inhabitants," the ancient Cushite empire of Ethiopians that covered three continents and held unbroken sway for three thousand years, had long passed the glorious era of its superior civilization; for indeed, the testimony and evidence of honest scholarship attests to the undeniable fact that the Cushite Ethiopians were the founders of primaeval cities and civilized life. They were emphatically the monument builders on the plains of Shinar and the valley of the Nile from Meroe to Memphis. This black or dark colored race were the pioneers of our civilization and although the Egyptian and Chaldean civilizations are very old, the culture and political organization of Ethiopia was much older. They belonged to what those same Egyptians and Chaldeans regarded as real antiquity, ages shrouded in doubt because they were so remote.

The Greeks looked to old Ethiopia and called the Upper Nile

the common cradle of mankind, and it was towards the rich luxuriance of this region that they looked for the "Garden of Eden". Arid in those primitive days, the central seat of Ethiopia was not the Meroe that we know of today, and which is very ancient, but a kingdom that preceded it by many ages that was called Meru. And in the sacred books of India, the Sanskrit writers called Indra, chief god of the Hindu, king of Meru; he was deified and became the chief representative of the supreme being. Thus, primitive India was settled by colonists from Ethiopia, and according to early writers there was very little difference in the color or features of the people of the two countries.

The early prosperity and grandeur of Ethiopia sprang from the trading along caravan routes between India and Arabia on the one hand, and the interior of Africa and Egypt on the other. This "merchandise of Ethiopia" of which the Bible so often speaks, through legendary cities like Axum, Meroe, Thebes, Carthage and Adulis, was how Egypt obtained the immense quantities of spices and drugs with which she embalmed her dead, as well as the costly incense that burned on her altars, and the enormous amount of cotton in which her inhabitants were clad. All the gold, ebony, ivory were provided to Egypt and the Mediterranean by this international commerce of which Ethiopia of old was the center and seat.

The ancient greatness of Ethiopia is undeniable, even apart from the evidence of Archaeology and History, especially if we consider the substantial demand for incense which provided the fabulous wealth that she was known for. These precious substances were used not only for embalming the dead, but also to allay the odours of animal sacrifices, and in ancient times when the dead were buried in churches, the burning of incense was thought necessary to preserve the health of mourners. All this gives us a faint idea of how enormous was the traffic to supply such demands. So then, when we consider the precious, natural products of Ethiopia, her commerce, the strength of her armies, which Scriptures mentions as a thousand thousand, there is surely a substantial foundation for the many traditions of ancient greatness about her.

Although for centuries within fairly modern times they were almost forgotten by Europe, the Ethiopians were familiar to the peoples of the Near and Middle East from prehistoric times and throughout the Christian era, as an independent Christian empire which was of the family of the ancient non-Roman and non-European civilized world.

The wars of invasion which repeatedly ravaged Ethiopia destroyed the greater part of her early achievements; and her rich history, often fraught with heroism and peril, and often disturbed by the numerous invasions which has ruthlessly obliterated much of the earlier glories of Ethiopian genius, resulted inevitably in a sad impoverishment from which nevertheless she has always risen, again and again, after every reverse however terrible.

For the Ethiopian people, their unique traditions and history always provided them with a source of renewing strength and hope, to which in the midst of overwhelming tragedies and measureless disasters she could always turn to, and imbibe in the glories of far gone eras when the cultural hegemony of the realm extended far beyond the known frontiers of the modern day kingdom.

And so it is, that among the many traditions that make up the extensive iconography and symbols of the Ethiopian nation, the fascinating epic narrated in the sacred book KEBRA NAGAST "The Glory of Kings" is at the center of the soul of the nation, and truly revered by its dark-skinned subjects.

The KEBRA NAGAST is old and the story it tells is even older; and in Ethiopia it is of great political importance. Upon the legends of the KEBRA NAGAST is based the right of the Kings of Ethiopia to rule their subjects, who have been independent since the days of the Old Testament. During most of its millennarian history the ancient kingdom has been cut off from the rest of the world by the towering, magnificent and frightening mountains that make up a good share of the country.

The story which is told in the KEBRA NAGAST and which school boys and girls in Ethiopia learn along with the ABC's of the strange Amharic alphabet, tells of the Queen of Sheba, the Queen of Ethiopia, who had heard of the might and wisdom of King Solomon, ruler of the Land of the Jews. She was determined to see for herself the magnificence and splendour of Solomon's kingdom, and she journeyed from her own country to his royal court, bearing many gifts, and armed with her own famous beauty, for she was then considered to be one of the most beautiful women in the world.

She was not disappointed, for all that she had heard of the glory of Solomon's court was true. He was indeed the greatest of all the kings in the world and the Queen of Sheba remained at his side, asking for his advice, so that she could return to her own country and govern with equal wisdom and splendour.

Solomon would gladly have made her his queen, for he was delighted by her beauty and grace, but she felt that her duty demanded that she remain with her own people. However, for a time she did become the companion of King Solomon and she bore him a son. According to the KEBRA NAGAST, this was Solomon's first-born son. He was named Bayna Lekem, meaning "son of the wise man", and his father gave him a notable jeweled ring by means of which he could prove to the world his descent from the ruler of the Land of the Jews.

In Ethiopia, Bayna Lekem assumed the throne name of Menyelek I and ascended the throne that was abdicated in his favor by his mother, the Queen of Sheba. And so was established the line of kings of the Royal House of David and Solomon in Ethiopia, reputed to be the oldest monarchy in the world. To the young child, Bayna Lekem, as heir to the throne, special attention was given to his education and training which was to prepare him for his future responsibilities; most of his childhood and early manhood was spent in the seclusion of a mountain peak, where under the careful guidance of learned sages and specially selected tutors he received the necessary learning suited to a Prince of such exalted ancestry.

Undoubtedly, the crowning achievement of this great monarch, the first in a long line of blood-related kings of the Solomonic line in Ethiopia, was the bringing forth of the Holy Ark of the Covenant from Jerusalem to Ethiopia, which signified the transfer of Israel and the physical presence of God to its new abode within the "land where the God's love to be". And King Menyelek I, armed with the supernatural might and power of the Sacred Ark of God, made war on the host of the enemies and idolaters, and laid waste the countries round about that had refused to recognize the supremacy of the King of Ethiopia and did not render obeisance to him, nor paid tribute to his majestic order.

And so King Menyelek I, extended the frontiers of the realm and made the kingdom great; and all the nations around bowed down low before his dreadful majestic power, for they saw that the awesomeness of God and the invincible might of the Ark of the Covenant were with him, and they feared the overwhelming superiority of his chariots and the skill of his numerous horsemen and his soldiers.

The genealogy of the kings of Ethiopia were chronicled in many ancient holy books such as the Serata-Mangest or "Order of the Realm" and in the "Book of Axum" where it shows that Kush the son of Shem, begot Ityopis the father of Aksumawi whose offspring became the founders of the holy city of Aksum. And after King Menyelek I, comes King Gedur of the city of Nouh, and later when Ethiopia ruled even unto Meroe, Nubia and Egypt, many great kings continued the monumental works of their ancestors, and were known as the Ethiopian dynasty from the south, the twenty-fifth which ruled Egypt between 751 and 656 B.C. and which included the reigns of Piankhy, Shabaka and Taharka. This dynasty had then retired to the depths of Nubia, where it established in the kingdom of Meroe in the course of the next thousand years, an artistic and religious culture which became increasingly cut off from that of Egypt.

Thus, far back in antiquity, the record of various regional kingdoms and principalities which frequently changed borders and rulership, display a consistent genealogy of the blessed seed and this becomes evident to the discerning and persistent enquirer.

Then, at about the middle of the first century A.D. a Graeco-Egyptian author wrote the celebrated *Periplus of the Erythraean Sea* where detailed references are made of Zoscales, King of Aksum, who already had an extensive area under his direct control; he dispatched caravans to distant destinations beyond Lake Tana, and his trading representatives were in commercial relations with Egypt by way of the Nile.

The first recorded appearance of the imperial title King of Kings was with Sembruthes of Aksum, and this was at about the second or third century A.D. by which time Aksum enjoyed a powerful position due to her control of the Red Sea, Arabia and Nubia. His successors, King Afilas, Endybis and Wazeb I, established their sovereignty more effectively than ever, consolidating the growing influence of the Aksumite empire in the region.

Following in the line of notable and illustrious Aksumite kings, the name of King Ella-Amida appears as the one responsible for the overthrow of the kingdom of Meroe; his rule ended around the year 323 A.D. and his son, who succeeded him, is regarded as one of the greatest of the Ethiopian emperors of antiquity; his name was Ezana. At the start of his reign he was still a minor, and his mother acted as regent. The reign of King Ezana was to be distinguished by the conversion of the sovereign himself, and later on of the empire, to Christianity.

It was during his remarkable rulership that Ezana embarked on numerous campaigns in defence of his realm and to unify Ethiopia, thereby safeguarding the routes which meant everything to her prosperity. The inscriptions upon the many stelae memorializing the military victories of his armies, uses only one language, archaic Geez, the script of which must have been in existence for a long time, but, so far, had never been used for official purposes. These evidenced the religious conversion of the Emperor, since his successes were dedicated to the LORD OF HEAVEN AND EARTH, indicating the advent of Christianity in Ethiopia.

The reign of Ezana brought about the final assimilation of the Arabian invaders and their culture, as well as the absorption of certain Hellenistic elements by the empire, and the eventual peaceful consolidation of the kingdom in an inhospitable land, against the inroads of many disinherited tribes and principalities. All these factors, along with the introduction of a religion, language and a form of writing along with the unification and organization of the empire, culminated in the formation of the Ethiopian nation with its unique and remarkable individuality in the annals of history.

After Ezana several monarchs appear on the scene; these are Wazeb II, Eon, Alalmisyisis and Wasas. These prepare the way for the legendary conqueror King Kaleb (ruled 514-542 A.D.) who as emperor had sent an expedition to assist the Christians of Himyar in South Arabia who were suffering the dreadful persecutions of the governor Dhu Nuwas.

Dhu Nuwas was an Arab who had been appointed as governor by the Emperor; there he embarked on the most grievous and cruel campaign against the Christians of the area, prompting protests from Timothy, Patriarch of Alexandria. It was especially in the city of Nagran that he displayed the most heineous and bestial opposition to Christians by the martyrdom of Saint Aretas, and the massacring of 340 other believers by burning them to death in pits of fire. The Emperor sent 323 ships and 120,000 men to aid the distressed Christians. Dhu Nuwas was speedily vanquished, and being wounded by the Emperor himself, he rode his horse into the sea and was drowned. Having assured the safety of the Christian population in Southern Arabia, the Emperor established two governors to maintain order in the Arabian territories. Thus, the prestige of the Aksumite empire increased to such extent that it came to be regarded by the Byzantine world as one of the champions of Christianity.

At around this time, between the years 540 and 580 AD, the Persian fleets that were marauding the opposite shores of the Red Sea, gained supremacy in the area and Ethiopia started losing control and influence in Arabia. Suddenly the Aksumite empire found itself deprived not only of its overseas territory, but also of its commercial outlets since the merchant ships were unable to pass beyond the Babel-Mandeb strait.

With this unfortunate crippling of her seaports, Ethiopia hoped to survive by developing other trade routes, but the growth of Islam which had cut off Egypt from the Byzantine sphere, had also brought about the gradual isolation of Ethiopia from all Mediterranean contact. The only relations now open to Ethiopia were therefore with Islam, still in its infancy. Initially these relations went fairly well. In the year 615 A.D., the prophet Mohammed told a group of his companions that were fleeing from the persecutions of the opposing Quraishites, that they should take refuge at the court of Aksum, for "When you go into Abyssinia, you will find there a king under whom no man is persecuted. It is a land of justice, where God will bring you rest from your tribulations." And the strangers were indeed made welcome, and they afterwards returned to their city in Arabia filled with wonder and awe at the beauty of the Ethiopian churches.

Later however, the fairly good harmony existing between Arabia and Ethiopia suffered a setback when piratical attacks coming from the Aksumite Port against the Arab bases located on the opposite bank of the Red Sea, went unpunished by the Ethiopian authorities. These attacks went on from the years 640 right up to 702 when a major assault was made on Jeddah. The Moslems had no choice but to retaliate by capturing Massawa, the Dahlak Islands, and destroying the legendary port of Adulis by fire. Eventually the Aksumites were driven from the whole coastal area and reduced to the status of a virtual political nonentity. This was a disaster from which they never fully recovered.

In little over one hundred years the empire had passed from untold power and prosperity, to a state of utter desolation, as Ethiopia now found herself suddenly isolated from the Christian world and also from the civilized world of which she had become an integral part after centuries of firm progress in both, domestic and foreign affairs. And so it was, that among both, Ethiopian and Moslems, it was prophesied that one day Ethiopia the indomitable, would arise and destroy Mecca, for as the psalmist said, "Ethiopia shall stretch her hands unto God," and deliver the world.

There are certain Apocaliptic writings dating to the seventh century compiled by two illustrious monks, Pisenios of Thebes and Samuel of Qalamun, where they prophesied to suffering Christians everywhere that the Emperor of Ethiopia would once again unite with the Emperor of Rome, and that together they would vanquish Islam.

Thus, from the seventh to the twelfth century, Ethiopia remained essentially cut off from the rest of the world. Facing her, was a life of isolation and austerity, mirroring perhaps the voluntary solitude of the countless monks who dwell in silence and inward contemplation, in the recesses of her ever present mountains.

Then there came about a kind of retreat inland, away from the plateau of Tigre province towards the mountainous center of the kingdom, where several principalities, among them the realms of Lasta, Shoa, Gojjam and Amhara united in the task of restoring the ancient traditions, stimulating a rich rebirth of the arts and literature, along with a consolidation of territorial unity within Ethiopia. This lengthy era of virtual silence in the long and turbulent history of Ethiopia, is one about which not much is known. Those were five hundred years in which the enigmatic trajectory of the Blessed Seed of Solomon, coursed in its relentless path through the blood of the Ethiopian Princes of the tribe of Israel, towards the prophetic destiny that would be fulfilled in the last days.

While this great renaissance in the religious, artistic and literary life of the kingdom flourished unto the twelfth century, certain tumultuous events emerged, that would permanently mark its imprint in the character and the life of the nation. As the Royal Ethiopian Chronicles state it... "Now it came to pass that the kingdom passed to another people who were not of the tribe of Israel... these people were called the *Zagwe...*" This royal line was of ancient Agaw blood, which originated in the district of

Bugna, and they established their claim to the throne through the marriage of one of their princes to the daughter of one of the last rulers of Aksum, Delnaad. The new non-Solomonic dynasty which they established in the heart of the Lasta province mountains, remained in power and eventually was recognized by the Ethiopian church.

And even though this dynasty of the usurping *Zagwe* kings was not of the race of David, they claimed descent from Moses, who had married the daughter of an ancient king of the land. The throne of David was theirs, claimed the *Zagwe* emperors, who also claimed the priesthood through descendance from Aaron, first high priest of Israel. But the Ethiopians had the Holy Ark of the Covenant which was with them from the days of King Menyelek I. It was only on the great feast days that it was brought out and carried in procession, with an escort of young Israelites of the race of David.

Three were the outstanding kings of the *Zagwe* dynasty: Imraha, Naakueto Laab, and Lalibela. Undoubtedly, the greatest achievements of the *Zagwe* era took place during the reign of Lalibela, in the form of various political reforms, and above all, the establishment of the famous sanctuaries of Roha and the building of the remarkable and marvellous monolithic churches built in the town that was named after him, Lalibela.

These extraordinary churches are true monoliths, hewed and carved out of the living rock using a technique of the most advanced architectural skill. The means required to work the massive rock had to be of an incredibly high order, one that could only be imitated today with the use of reinforced concrete.

Lalibela's new capital seemed to have been an attempt to replace the ancient city of Aksum as the holy city of the Ethiopians. Yet, in spite of the profound sanctity and piety displayed by the rulers in their impassioned faith, their dynasty was doomed to be a relatively short-lived one. For there emerged an Amhara prince named Yekuno Amlak who incited a successful rebellion in the province of Shoa, that spread throughout the realm and gained support with a powerful sector of the church. Later on, the reigning *Zagwe* king was driven out of his capital and murdered in Gaint.

The emergence of the *Zagwe* kings in Ethiopia was preceded by an extraordinary period of internecine wars and upheavals in the Central Ethiopian Highlands, and which spread to other areas of the kingdom. As it is recorded in the "Book of Saints of the Ethiopian Church," a warrior-queen of the Agaw, known as Esat (fire) or Judith and who was of the Jewish faith was ravaging the country, burning the churches and slaughtering the clergy and the people. According to Ethiopian tradition Judith was desirous of exterminating the Christian dynasty, and had sacked Aksum and cast down most of the monolithic towers there.

As a result of the murderous scorched-earth campaigns of the feared Agaw queen, all the members of the reigning dynasty were murdered save one child, who was conveyed to Shoa, one of the ancient kingdoms of the Ethiopian Federation under the King of Kings. This young scion of the Royal House of Israel was cherished by the Lords of the Kingdom, who were most passionately zealous in their loyalty to the Solomonic dynasty.

From Ethiopian sources it is stated that this royal child was the young emperor Anbasa Weddem, and that after living for some years in Shoa, he regained the throne at Aksum. Following the overthrow of the government at Aksum, the descendants of the Solomonic line continued their rule in Shoa.

Meanwhile, when the son of Emperor Anbasa Weddem, Delnaad, was reigning, Takla Haymanot, Governor of Lasta who was his son-in-law, killed him and seized the kingdom and ruled under the name Zawege. His successors on the throne were Janseyum, Germaseyum, Gampawedamo, Yemreha, Gabre Mariam, Lalibela, Naakuto Laab and Yetbarik. Of these, Naakuto Laab was said to be wild and licentious in his youth, but was stricken with remorse when, because of his evil life, the daughter of Lalibela committed suicide rather than marry him.

It was on the advice of the Ethiopian saint, Takla Haymanot

(not Zawege, above noted) that Naakuto Laab abdicated the throne in favour of Yekuno Amlak, a member of the Solomonic dynasty who was then ruling in Shoa.

Takla Haymanot the saint, is regarded with enormous gratitude and reverence in Ethiopia, as the major influence in restoring the traditional Solomon dynasty. This most famous of Ethiopian saints was a descendant of Zadok the High Priest of Jerusalem, who, along with Nathan the Prophet had anointed Solomon as King of Judah and Israel. The eldest son of Zadok, Azariah, was one of the band of young priests and nobles who accompanied Menyelek I, son of Solomon and the Queen of Sheba, on his return to his mother in Ethiopia after his historic visit to King Solomon in Jerusalem.

Having been appointed a deacon at the age of fifteen, Takla Haymanoth, whose name means "Tree of the Faith", subsequently became head of the Ethiopian Church, and afterwards spent many years as a hermit in the desert, and died at the age of 91 years.

With the reign of Yekuno Amlak, whose name is by interpretation "to him shall be sovereignty" (1268-1283), the dynasty that came out of Israel was thus restored to the throne, with its line of kings traditionally descended from Solomon as maintained by the Chronicles. The celebrated historical work known as the KEBRA NAGAST (The Glory of Kings) was already in existence then, but it was during the reign of Yekuno Amlak that it was officially codified with the objective of proving the descent of this Solomonic line of kings, and has remained in its present form ever since as the official documentary evidence for the Ethiopian royal succession. Furthermore, the systematic recording of the Royal Chronicles of Ethiopia, wherein the principal events of each reign were rewritten, began at this time.

The accession of Yekuno Amlak to the throne of the restored Solomon dynasty, signalled the beginning of a period of rapid development which was to continue for another two hundred years. During this time there was a great revival in Ethiopia under a series of rulers who were scholars as well as warriors. Territorial unity was once more established, civil and religious institutions were rigorously codified, and literature and art began to flourish again.

The restoration of the Israelite dynasty of the Royal House of David and Solomon in Ethiopia, signified the reaffirmation of the generally misunderstood Davidic Covenant as outlined in scriptures.

For, when David was king over Israel and Judah, God made with him an absolutely binding, unconditional and perpetual covenant which the almighty will not and can not break.

And it came to pass that night, that the word of the Lord came unto Nathan, saying, "Go and tell my servant David, Thus saith the Lord... When thy days be fulfilled, and thou shalt sleep with thy fathers, I will set up thy seed after thee, which shall proceed out of thy bowels (Solomon), and I will establish his kingdom. He shall build a house for my name, *and I will establish the throne of his kingdom for ever*. I will be his father, and he shall be my son. If he commit iniquity, I will chasten him with the rod of men, and with the stripes of the children of men: But my mercy shall not depart away from him... *And thine house and thy kingdom shall be established for ever* before thee: THY THRONE SHALL BE ESTABLISHED FOR EVER" (II Samuel 7:4-5, 12-16).

So then, David's throne was set up and established *forever* in Solomon, David's son, unconditionally guaranteeing that there should never be a single generation from that time forward when there would not be a descendant of David, *in unbroken dynasty* sitting on David's throne. The royal history in the Bible records a line of kings, all descendants of David in continuous dynasty, down to King Zedekiah. But in the year 585 B.C. this last recorded king ever to sit on this throne was captured by the armies of King Nebuchadnezzar of Babylon, his eyes were gouged out, he was taken to Babylon, and there died in a dungeon. Moreover, all his sons were slain! Every one of the nobles of Judah who was not already imprisoned or enslaved at Babylon at that time, was

43

killed, so that none could remain to sit on the throne of David. The Babylonians had destroyed Jerusalem, sacked and burned the Temple and the king's palaces, and took the Jews as captives, to Babylon. So, the royal line of Judah ended there, for Christ, who was also of the royal lineage of David, did not sit on the throne of David at his first advent but would do so at his second coming.

The messianic promises in Jeremiah chapter 33, prophecy of events to occur at the time of Christ's coming in supreme power and glory. "Behold the days come, saith the Eternal, that I will perform that good thing which I have promised *unto the house of Israel and to the house of Judah*" (Jeremiah 33:14). "In those days shall Judah be saved and Jerusalem shall dwell safely... For thus saith the Eternal; David shall never want a man to sit *upon the throne of the house of Israel (*Jeremiah 33:16-17). And God *did* establish that throne beginning with David and Solomon, but the promise was given unto *both houses,* Judah and Israel. And there has been since that time, a descendant of the lineage of David sitting upon a royal throne, either of Judah or of Israel.

The eternal covenant remained, and the transfer of God's Holy Ark of the Covenant from Jerusalem to Ethiopia, ensured that the royal and sacred blood of David would continue there, manifested in the Dynasty of the Blessed Seed, the line of Solomonic Kings of Ethiopia.

As a descendant of this Solomonic line, Yekuno Amlak, having resided in Shoa for most of his life, spoke his native tongue, Amharic, the language of Amhara and Shoa, which by this time diverged considerably from the ancient Geez; so Amharic, being the language of the Imperial Court, became the most widely diffused Ethiopian language.

Under Yekuno Amlak's successor Yagbea Seyon (1285-1294) the incipient encroachments of Islamic immigrants to the coastal regions started developing into a virtual invasion, until the full weight of their hostility against the Christian kingdom, emerged in all the bitterness of a holy war. Meanwhile in Egypt, the Muslims had begun to persecute the Coptic Christians and to destroy their churches. It was Emperor Amda Seyon "Pillar of Zion" (1314-1344) who demanded restoration of the churches destroyed, with the threat that failure to do so would result in diversion of the Nile waters and the consequent starvation of Egypt, and reprisals against any Moslem who entered the realm. Not only did his ambassador return without the required undertaking, but his lands were raided by the Sultan of Ifat, who proceeded to burn down the churches and to compel the people to embrace Islam, and murdering an ambassador from the king also in the bargain.

Emperor Amda Seyon's reaction was swift and fulminating, stimulating a glorious revival in Ethiopian prestige. In the year 1328 he conquered Ifat and Fatajar appointing as governor there, the brother of the defeated Sultan; but the new leader betrayed him by seeking an alliance against him with the Jewish section of the Agaw population from the northern regions of Lake Tana. This rebellion was quickly foiled by Amda Seyon who laid waste the lands of Hadya, Fatajar and Dawaro; and he placed them under the control of yet another brother of the two sultans he had overthrown.

The Ethiopia over which he reigned was essentially a collection of small states with no definite seat of government, apart from the sacred city of Aksum and several royal residences scattered throughout the realm. But in religion, art and political organization the country was steadily going forward, and learned scholars began to revise the Aksumite translations from the Scriptures, while the texts for numerous rites and liturgies were transcribed in Geez for the first time. The monastic brethren however, had displayed a vexatious spirit towards Amda Seyon, because he had taken as wives his father's harem of concubines, a practice which was rather common at the time. Consequently, Abba Honorius proceeded to excommunicate him, but the emperor retaliated by condemning the monk as a heretic, having him flogged in public at the market place, and subjecting the religious community at the monastery of Debra-Libanos in Shoa to an ignominious exile.

During this period, no effort was spared to convert the heathen, thereby incorporating into the kingdom, tribes not hitherto under their full control. In this mission, the spiritual inheritors of the great monks Takla Haymanot and Eustathius won special distinctions. Eustathius, who died somewhere around the middle of the fourteenth century, was particularly zealous in his evangelizing endeavours, being responsible for the destruction of a number of sacred trees and pagan shrines which he reduced to ashes.

Eustathius was famous for the extremes he went to in the showy display of self-flagellation and the terrifying mortification of the flesh which he frequently inflicted upon his body. "Fetch me some chains," he said one day to one of his disciples. "And leave them in the sun until they are red-hot!" The saintly monk then tied himself up with the burning chains binding them around his neck, arms and feet until his skin blistered and he resembled, in the words of the text, "a fish grilled in the fire". He was a fanatical pilgrim who could inspire his followers to emulate his penchant for many unnecessary forms of self-inflicted tortures, ostensibly for the purpose of mitigating the condemnatory effects of real or imagined sins against the deity.

The international prestige that Ethiopia had by now acquired was such, that during the reign of Sayfa Arad (1344-1372) she took on the role of official protector of the Patriarchy of Alexandria, so that in 1352 she avenged the imprisonment of the Patriarch Mark by either executing or forcibly converting all Egyptian merchants found on Ethiopian territory. After these dramatically persuasive episodes, relations with Egypt improved considerably, to the extent that the succeeding Emperor, David I (1382-1411), welcomed at his court an ambassador of Egypt, sending in return twenty-two camels loaded with gifts for the Sultan Barquk. Later on, he obtained from Jerusalem a portion of the "True Cross of Christ" and a number of precious religious paintings including the famous *Kuerata Reesu,* which depicts the figure of Christ crowned with thorns, and to which many great miracles are attributed.

46

The brief reign of Theodore I (1414) deserves, special mention due to a curious piece of literary work of a prophetic nature entitled *FEKARE IYESUS* or Prophecy of Jesus, in which Christ is supposed to tell the Apostles about a king who will rise in the East, whose name is Theodore, and who will bring back peace and abundance to the world. Theodore, however, reigned only nine months, and so, this revelation of a world to come was henceforth a vision to stir the hearts of all who yearned for the advent, in a not-too-distant future, of a miraculous king in the land of Ethiopia....

Then there emerged one of the greatest rulers of the Solomonic dynasty, Zara Yaqob, whose name means "Seed of Jacob" (ruled 1434-1468) who undertook the formidable task of consolidating and unifying the Ethiopian territory and propagating the Christian faith, and in addition, he established and administered a strict code of laws that governs the life of Ethiopia unto this day. Zara Yaqob devoted himself not only to spreading Christianity, which he imposed by force upon the pagan peoples of Gojjam and Damot, but also to a series of intensive reforms at home amongst his own Christian subjects. He issued a decree ordering everyone to bear on his forehead and arms the affirmation of his faith, and the renunciation of the Devil, these, in the form of tatoo markings. All practitioners of the magical arts were denounced, and feast days and periods of fasting were established. The emperor also decreed that the Saturday, or seventh-day Sabbath, was to be kept holy, a regulation which was much criticised as being a form of 'Judaism', to the extent that it caused a revolt among the monks at the monastery of Debra-Libanos. The decree, however, stated that anyone who did not conform, even if it happened to be the King's own son, was punished without mercy.

The reign of Zara Yaqob coincided with a long struggle against heresy, and the beginnings of the great theological disputes which has since raged at intervals in Ethiopia. The king took a very active part in these religious controversies, and his known fear of spirits and sorcerers stimulated him to become a great religious writer. Among his numerous works is the *Matshafa Berhan* or

"Book of the Light" a collection of religious precepts; and under his guidance, the "Miracles of the Holy Virgin Mary" was translated from the Latin and Coptic writings. Other books of revelations were compiled, like the curious work "Book of the Mystery of Heaven and Earth," and a veritable proliferation of occult literature of diverse origin began to appear in great profusion, such as cabalistic works of a kind which have always been in great demand in Ethiopia. In these writings the innumerable secret names of God and Jesus are revealed, as well as magical spells and incantations along with astrological formulas. Other curious works include the apocryphal "Book of Enoch" and the Lefafa Sedek or "Bandlet of Truth", which was a set of magical prayers written on a roll of parchment which could then be buried with the deceased.

It was during the reign of Zara Yakob that the beginnings of diplomatic relations with the rulers of Europe were initiated, with a proposed alliance with Spain and Alfonso of Aragon being advanced as well as requests for safe-conduct of Ethiopian monks from Jerusalem through the Principalities of Venice and Florence in Italy. Zara Yakob died in 1468 and was buried near Lake Tana. His achievements were great in every field, for, in addition to his important work in the cultural sphere, he reorganized the administration of the provinces and restored order in the disturbed areas. He left behind him an Empire which extended from the Baraka river and Massaua down to Ifat, Fatajar and Bali, thereby giving the geographic boundaries of the empire a configuration very similar to the ones we know today.

At this time in the turbulent history of the Ethiopian nation, the intensification of the epic struggle with Islam brought about indelible changes in the life of the realm; deep transformations which resulted from the formidable clash of two emerging world religions vying for the hearts and minds of a naturally mystic and pious people. Zara Yakob's successor Baeda Mariam "In the Hand of Mary" (1468-1478) did not have to confront the fanatical Muslim warriors, but rather took advantage of a semblance of truce to launch terrible onslaughts against the Falasha Jews of the Lake

Tana region, who were challenging his authority and the emerging Christian faith of the kingdom.

When Baeda Mariam died, his wife Eleni became Regent for his young son Iskander who reigned briefly, and thereafter, the Empress Eleni was again Regent for 'Lebna Denghel "Incense of the Virgin", also known as Wanag Seged (1508-1540) who succeeded to the throne when only eleven years of age. According to ancient Ethiopian custom the elder queen reigned during the minority of the King.

Up to this time, according to the Royal Ethiopian Chronicles, Ethiopia had never been dismembered nor invaded by any enemy, but the invasion of the country by enemies began under King Lebna Denghel, the son of King Naod. His father, Naod, had enjoyed a peaceful reign (1494-1508), but his wife, the Empress Eleni, who was possessed of great wisdom, lived on until 1520, and did much to enhance the prestige of Ethiopia among the Western powers. She proved to be possessed of sound political judgment and a detailed knowledge of contemporary affairs, establishing and maintaining diplomatic relations with far-off countries, and demonstrating the extraordinary part played by women in the affairs of Christian Ethiopia.

Just as in the distant past, when Ethiopia appeared to the West as the mighty Empire of Aksum, now at the beginning of the sixteenth century she had suddenly become the embodiment of the fabulous and legendary kingdom of Prester John, which was sought by pilgrims since the days of the Crusades all over Central Asia and India, until eventually on the basis of more precise information, it was decided that Africa would be a more likely location to the mystery of the elusive Christian monarch. Thus, it was amidst these historical circumstances that the first Portuguese mission arrived in the Kingdom of Ethiopia after sailing down the coast of the Red Sea, emulating the great Persian, Greek, Egyptian and Arab navigators of bygone eras.

The Portuguese mission which arrived in Ethiopia in the year 1520 and remained there for seven years, had brought the first real ambassador to set foot on Ethiopian soil.

And in those days, this was truly an astounding event, both for Europe as well as for Ethiopia.

They were visiting Ethiopia on the appeal of the Dowager Empress, Eleni, who was anxious to strengthen the kingdom against the Turkish-Arab menace by forging an alliance with the friendly European Christian power. Father Francisco Alvarez, the Chaplain of this first Portuguese mission to Ethiopia, was the first European to write a substantial and accurate account of Ethiopian affairs.

As a priest, Alvarez was very impressed by the vast number of churches and the reverence in which they were held by the population at large, as well as the devotion and austerity of the Ethiopian clergy. The Portuguese were hoping to simultaneously effect a military alliance with Ethiopia and her conversion to Roman Catholicism, but as fate would have it, great troubles were brewing among the Moslem tribes of Danakil and Somalia, those turbulent and intractable nomads that were continually pressing upon the territorial coasts of Ethiopia.

These tribes found a champion in a leader who was totally different to the many ineffectual secular administrators who could not meet their aspirations; for their new man was revered as a saint or a prophet, since he was the *Imam* of the faithful, who immediately after coming to power slew the Sultan and thus secured supreme authority. His name was Ahmed Gran of Harar, and he promptly organized his forces, rallying large numbers of fanatical Somali warriors who launched a devastating holy war against Christian Ethiopia which began in 1528 and ended in 1542.

The destruction was by all accounts most terrible. Crops could not be cultivated and so, whole districts starved, and, as it was not safe to light a fire lest it attract a marauding party, the practice of eating meat raw resulted. Innumerable monasteries and churches were sacked and burned to the ground, and ancient manuscripts, icons and other works of art were stolen or destroyed. In the north, the wonderful old church at Aksum, where the Ethiopian monarchs had for centuries been crowned, was razed to the ground, and in the south the famous monastery of Debra Libanos was entirely demolished.

According to Gran's own chronicler, the horrendous record of reprehensible vandalism that punctuated the Imam's visceral hatred of all things Christian, knew no parallels. After his decisive victory and occupation of Dawaro, Shoa, Amhara and Lasta, and the wiping out of the Christian population of Kambata, Gran proceeded to destroy one by one the treasures of Ethiopia accumulated over the centuries by her great rulers; monuments and priceless objects whose magnificence would be forever lost to the world.

The same chronicler relates that the church of *Atronsa Maryam,* "Throne of Mary", was pillaged from midday till the following morning.

As Gran and his companions penetrated into it with great admiration, their contemplation of the fabulous interior almost caused them to lose the power of sight, for the entire inner walls were covered with sheets of gold and silver, upon which had been placed incrustations of pearls. The ceiling and the interior courts were covered with sheets of gold and ornamented with golden statues. The Moslems were amazed at the exquisite artistic work. They all crowded in, and Gran said unto them: "What any man takes shall be for himself, except for the sheets." They at once set to work with a thousand axes, tearing down the gold and also the incrustations which were inside the church. The invaders tore out rich brocaded silks and velvets, gold and silver in heaps, gold cups, plates and censers, a gold *tabot* on four legs weighing over a thousand ounces, an illuminated Bible bound in sheets of gold, and innumerable other riches.

When they were exhausted of collecting such a vast loot, they set fire to the church burning it down to the ground. Some of the monks were so grief stricken that they threw themselves into the flames and perished therein. In their savage sweep through the Ethiopian countryside, no church, sanctuary or monastery was spared, and they put to the sword a great number of Christians, and took into bondage many youths and nubile maidens and chil-

51

dren of both sexes who were then sold into the most abject slavery.

These were truly victorious conquerors on a fearsome mission that was fired by their compelling religious fanaticism. The entire fabric of Ethiopian civilization was being furiously destroyed by the implacable scourge of Gran's Moslem hordes.

After they had pillaged and destroyed Debra Libanos they proceeded south to Biet –Amhara, an area that possessed numerous sanctuaries and churches housing priceless treasures belonging to both Church and State. As the Moslem chronicler informs us, the famous Church of the Holy Trinity Makana-Selassie could be seen from afar as they approached, due to the gleaming gold that covered its outer walls and roof. The whole of the interior right up to the ceiling, shone with gold and silver plaques inlaid with pearls and decorated with a profusion of figures of various kinds. They immediately plundered the whole place and then burnt it to the ground.

The plunderers then went on to loot the Church of Ganata-Maryam, "Paradise of Mary", where the royal insignia and various other treasures had been concealed, including the crowns and diadems of ancient kings, ceremonial mantles, and daggers. They also made off with a number of *tabots* which were a type of altar table peculiar to the Ethiopian Church; they were made of gold, and were so heavy that it took at least six men together to carry it. The entire area from Lake Haik to Aksum and across to Lake Tana was plundered, the faithful slaughtered and forcibly converted, as they went along. They never stopped until at length their leader was killed and they fled, but by then there was hardly anything left to destroy.

Ahmed Gran of Harar had invaded large areas of the kingdom and had driven Emperor Lebna Dengel from one province to the next. The king, admitting rather late indeed, that he required foreign help, sent an appeal to the King of Portugal who responded positively, and in 1541 Portuguese troops under the command of Christopher Da Gama landed in Massaua. They were well armed with cannons, muskets and an ample supply of side-arms. Lebna Dengel never saw the liberation that they helped to bring about, for 'he who twenty years before rode forth on horseback, crowned, and with an escort of chained lions, died twelve months before their arrival with hardly an attendant.'

He had fled to the monastery of Debra Damo where, embittered by his memories of defeat and remorse he lived out his last days. His son Galawdewos, also known as Claudius (1540-1559), reaped the benefit of a belated victory by the Portuguese with their Ethiopian allies who had by now gathered a very large army of Ethiopian volunteers. In a decisive battle on February 21, 1543 Gran's men were taken by surprise at Waina Daga and decimated, and he himself was killed by a musket ball. Deprived of their leader, the Moslem invaders scattered and fled, only to be pursued and hacked to pieces on the way.

Ethiopia had once more survived a severe and excruciating ordeal, and this time her own forces had proved insufficient to defend and deliver her from the Moslem occupation which had brought ruin on the country, both, materially and morally. But after sixteen years of almost continuous warfare, Galawdewos, of the royal bloodline of the Blessed Seed of David and Solomon, could now turn to the reorganization of the country and the reestablishment of the government and the arts of peaceful administration. The king was devoted to literature, and was said to be more learned than the most aged *debteras* (these were the sages of the Ethiopian Church, roughly equivalent to the Jewish Rabbis).

The Moslem Sultanate, however, had made a last bid for revenge before being completely defeated, and at the instigation of Gran's widow, the *Imam's* avenger Nur-al-Wazir retaliated by launching an invasion of Fatajar. Galawdewos met him with an army reinforced by monks and church dignitaries who were obviously not trained nor suited for the rigours of warfare. Furthermore, the battle took place on Good Friday, an unlucky day in the view of Christians, who fought badly. The King entered the fray for love of a woman whom he had taken from her previous husband, a priest, and racked by remorse at what he had done, he flung himself into the thick of the battle and was promptly slain and beheaded. His head was then taken to Harar and presented to the widow of the Imam, after which it was exhibited for three years on top of a pillar.

Galawdewos was succeeded on the throne by Minas (1559-1563) who had been taken prisoner by the Moslems in the course of an earlier battle, and held for many years at Harar. He inherited a difficult situation since two new foes of Ethiopia appeared on the scene, the Galla tribes and the Ottoman Turks. This double onslaught of the Turks and Gallas proved to be too much for Minas, and by the time of his death, the Gallas had overrun a third of the empire. Within fifty years Ethiopia had suffered more foreign invasions than ever before in her history, and although the reigns of Galawdewos and Lebna-Dengel saw the country's great churches, sanctuaries and countless treasures totally destroyed, creative activity did not come to an end, and new writings were soon appearing as before.

The kingdom was still surrounded by her enemies, but within the national territory she continued to develop, and one by one her adversaries gradually disintegrated or withdrew. This state of diminished danger was already evident during the reign of Sarsa-Dengel (1563-1597), a resolute conqueror who was vigorous and undaunted in the face of peril. When he assumed the imperial mantle, he was confronted with a realm of shifting frontiers and devastated towns and villages, and there was no accommodations fit for an emperor; such was the devastation that was visited upon his country by the Moslems.

In the early years of his reign he was threatened by a coalition of nobles who attempted to put another king on the throne, and although Sarsa-Dengel was at first obliged to flee before them, he was eventually able to eliminate them one by one, and with the army firmly under his control, he proceeded to restore order within the kingdom and strengthened his defences against the Galla tribes. He subdued the southern provinces, hacking to pieces the Moslem cavalry of the Prince of Hadya, so that not a man, nor a horse, nor a shred of armour remained.

Sarsa-Dengel was able to celebrate at Aksum a magnificent coronation ceremony in the traditional manner and was seated upon the 'Throne of David' where he was crowned and given his throne name of Malak-Sagad, meaning 'The Kings Adored Him'. After a reign of thirty-five years he had expelled the Turks, stopped the advance of the Galla tribes, extended the kingdom as far as the Kaffa region, and paved the way for the pacification of the realm. And so, Ethiopia, which at this time remained in effect liberated from her external enemies, seemed to be poised for a prolonged period of peace and consolidation. But the profound religious controversies that raged, at times violently, during the reign of his successor, divided the Ethiopians themselves into two theological camps of a deadly rivalry, which obviated for a considerable time any possibility of unity and harmony among the subjects of the millenarian mountain kingdom.

With the death of Malak-Sagad there came about a prolonged struggle for succession to the throne, a situation which was rather common, given the long history of intrigue and conflict which often resulted from opposing claims to the throne. This unsettled set of circumstances in the affairs of Ethiopian royalty were further exacerbated by the arrival in the country of one of the most accomplished and deviously cunning Roman Catholic Jesuit priest, Pedro Paez. His arrival on May 15, 1603 at Fremona, where the Portuguese Jesuits first settled in Ethiopia, signaled the start of profound changes in the character of the realm; changes which would have long-lasting effects upon the lives of its people, and greatly influence the course of events in the nation.

Father Paez was a Spaniard and a man of heroic stature, who had been sent as the newly appointed Patriarch of the Portuguese Roman Catholics in Ethiopia. He showed remarkable ability in the work of conversion, and though initially he was obliged to address congregations through an interpreter, he quickly became extraordinarily conversant not only with the Ethiopian language, but with the mentality of the people also. He had been sent to make renewed efforts to secure the submission of Ethiopian Christianity to the See of Rome.

55

The Ethiopian Emperor at the arrival of Pedro Paez in Ethiopia, was Jakob, a child of only thirteen years of age, and Paez lost no time in an effort to ingratiate himself with the young ruler, to whom he wrote, expressing the desire to kiss his hand. Jakob responded with a cordial invitation to the court, but before Paez arrived, Jakob was at war with his uncle Za Dengel, who had a better claim to the Imperial Throne, since he was nominated by the deceased Emperor Malak Sagad. The young Jakob was rapidly defeated, and Father Paez immediately transferred his attention to the victorious one.

Pedro Paez seem to have been an eloquent preacher, as well as a persistent advocate of the Roman Catholic Church. Born in 1564 of a noble Castillian family, his training as a Jesuit had rendered him most adept in the art of persuasion and diplomacy. His sermons were heard with effusive admiration both by the laity and clergy of Ethiopia, and after his second sermon, Paez was summoned by the Emperor to participate in the daily discussions of faith and doctrine, which continually took place at the palace in the presence of the monarch and the notables of the court.

Thus, Paez was rapidly gaining great influence at the Ethiopian Court, and whereas the Egyptian *Abunas* rarely acquired an adequate knowledge of *Geez* or *Amharic,* and were content to deliver their sermons in Arabic, Paez was diligently studying the Ethiopian languages. In his advocacy of the Roman Church and its doctrines, Paez was supported of course, by his long training as a Jesuit, but, still more, he was armed with a persuasive argument which he frequently dangled before the anxious mind of Atnaf Segged; the hope of an alliance with the powerful Christian kingdom of Spain, which would strengthen the Ethiopian monarchy against both external and internal foes, and would bring to Ethiopia the weapons and arts of Europe. Paez assured the young Emperor that a Spanish alliance was entirely within his reach, but on one condition only, the acknowledgement of the Pope of Rome as the Supreme Vice-Regent of God on Earth.

Under the strong and superior intellect of the mature and subtle

Jesuit, the young Emperor was soon induced to make formal submission to the Pope and to request a Spanish alliance. At first Atnaf Segged confided these intentions to Pedro Paez under the seal of secrecy, but being impatient to convert his country to the faith he had just been persuaded to espouse, he declared to Paez his intention to prohibit the observance of the Seventh Day Sabbath and to limit the weekly day of worship to Sunday, the Christian "First Day". Paez objected, saying that such a move would be premature, but the zealous young Emperor persisted in his decision.

It was therefore decided that Atnaf Segged should write to the Pope and to the King of Spain, and that Paez would have the letters conveyed secretly to them. The letters which were dated 26th of June 1604, carried a request from the Emperor to Pope Clement VIII, that Pedro Paez be confirmed as Ethiopian patriarch; and after expressing his desire for friendly relations with Spain, begged the Pope "to intercede with our brother, King Philip," to send soldiers without delay. To King Philip III he proposed a Spanish-Ethiopian alliance, to be cemented by the marriage of Philip's daughter, aged three years, to his own son aged seven. The letters, which were to prove the downfall of the young Emperor, were completed and dispatched, shortly after which, the news had leaked out that the Emperor had written to Spain for troops to enforce the Roman doctrines.

The Ethiopian people swiftly rebelled, and Za Sellassie, one of the counsellors who had assisted the Empress to govern the realm when Malak Segged died, had summoned a rebel army in defence of the Alexandrian faith, proclaiming his intention to depose Atnaf Segged and seat the young Jakob again upon the throne. Paez had advised the Emperor to find a safe sanctuary for the winter and leave the war to take its course, but instead, Atnaf Segged rode into battle himself and was killed on the 16th of October 1604, having reigned only one year.

Za Dengel, who had taken the name Atnaf Segged on ascending the Imperial Throne had shown strong leanings towards Roman Catholicism, and so, he was excommunicated by the *Abuna*

Petros, driven out by the nobles, and eventually died upon the battlefield and was left there without burial. Za Dengel's conversion to Catholicism had brought down on his head a storm of opposition which resulted in his eventual downfall.

There was now a struggle for the throne between the youthful ex-Emperor Jakob, and Susenyos, a great-grandson of the Emperor Lebna Dengel. He was also a cousin of the deceased Atnaf Segged, whom he had earlier supported in his fight to depose Jakob. Meanwhile, Father Pedro Paez, who had remained aloof from the storm he had brought upon Atnaf Segged, craftily decided not to support either Jakob or Susenyos, but rather to wait until the struggle between them was over and then "to take the side of the one who wins". Later on, the close relations which the young Jakob maintained with the Jesuits, caused large scale defections from his forces and led to his defeat and death in battle on the 4th of March, 1607.

Susenyos emerged then as the unchallenged claimant to the Imperial Throne, and by virtue of his unquestioned Solomonic blood-heritage was destined to receive the royal regalia, the crown and royal vestments, and the canopy of state. He at once took up official residence at Gubae, and in 1608, clothed in purple damask robes, with a golden chain about his neck, was crowned with due solemnity and ceremony at the ancient city of Aksum. Although Susenyos was more mature in years than the two young Emperors who had preceded him, he also was doomed to fall victim to the dangerous influence of the scheming Jesuit, Pedro Paez.

Born of the Imperial House in 1572, Susenyos had early in his life experienced adversity, as in the year following his birth the Gallas attacked his home and slew his father, Fasilidas. As a young babe, he himself was carried away by one of the Galla chieftains who proposed to raise him as his own son, but he was subsequently rescued and taken to the Empress Admas Mogasa, widow of the Emperor Minas, who received the orphan child with kindness and committed his education to a learned sage who taught him to read the Scriptures.

Paez wasted no time in advocating the Roman doctrines and in using the promise of a Spanish alliance which, though never to be realized, had its old fatal attraction for Susenyos, as it had for his two predecessors who had already fallen in the futile quest of this elusive dream. According to Paez's own account, by the year 1620 he had brought Emperor Susenyos to the state of mind in which he conceived it his imperative duty to abolish observance of the Seventh Day Sabbath. In that year, he tells us, the Emperor issued a decree announcing that land owners who allowed their labourers a holiday on Saturday, would suffer confiscation of their lands. This caused, as might have been anticipated, serious unrest and great indignation, especially since before this time, Paez had induced the Emperor to confer vast tracts of land upon the Roman Catholic priesthood.

Eventually, Susenyos disclosed to Father Paez that he was willing to write to the Pope recognizing his supremacy, but he desired also to write to King Philip of Spain for assistance in enforcing a change in religious doctrine, which he well knew would be intensely resented by large numbers of the Ethiopian people. Paez thereupon declared that if the Emperor would pay obedience to the Roman Church, he was convinced that the necessary soldiers would arrive. He then urged Susenyos to write to the Pope, the King of Spain and his Viceroy in India, and to convey the letters by an ambassador. Susenyos replied that he could not send an ambassador and requested that Paez send the letters secretly, just as his predecessors had done. The letters were finally written, but the difficulty facing the Ethiopian monarch and his advisors, was how to send these communications, since the Red Sea route was not feasible due to the presence of a powerful Turkish fleet controlling the entire coasts and sea lanes.

Then another Jesuit, Father Antonio Fernandez immediately proposed going overland to Melinde on the Zambesi delta where there were Portuguese settlements. This was a truly frightful journey of some 2,500 miles across unknown territory which would be enough to daunt anyone these days, yet to a Portuguese of that period there was nothing special about it. When he reached as far as Kaffa with his companions, they found the inhabitants, as in the days of Aksum, bartering their gold for basic commodities such as salt, livestock and clothing from the northern regions. Travelling laboriously into the depths of the African hinterland, they reached strange kingdoms where witchcraft was practiced by mysterious dark-skinned African kings whose aggressive subjects were given to cannibalistic endeavours, and so they were obliged to turn back.

In spite of this set back, and in spite of the numerous opponents who tried to get him publicly excommunicated by the *Abuna,* and the many attacks that were made on the Jesuits, such as a pamphlet which described them as the 'Children of Pontius Pilate', Susenyos stubbornly persisted in his purpose. He began by banning observance of the Sabbath, thereafter going to Father Paez for confession, thus demonstrating his conversion to the Catholic faith. Later on, his conversion was publicly announced at Aksum in a solemn proclamation before the elders, many of whom were already converted to the Roman religion. And in fact, there was significant response to the Jesuits among large numbers of the nobility, since the Catholic priesthood had the knack of putting over their religion in a way people could easily understand.

Paez had succeeded in converting Emperor Susenyos to the Roman Catholic faith in 1622. Undoubtedly his most important convert, this became his dying work as shortly afterwards he was seized by an undulating tropical fever brought on by overwork and exposure to the elements, and died at Gorgora in May of that year despite the attentions of his devoted companions.

Ethiopians revolted against a foreign religion being compulsorily introduced whether anyone liked it or not. The immediate measures that the Catholic clergy sought to impose were so uncompromising and onerous, that the general population found them to be unacceptable. All Christian Ethiopians had to be re-baptized and every church reconsecrated. In addition, the traditional *tabots* or Arks were prohibited, and the ancient liturgy in *Geez*, which was so highly revered, was summarily discarded in favour of the Latin mass which no one understood. They also denounced the cult of the Ethiopian saints, with many of their remains being disinterred and flung out of the sanctuaries after their tombs were desecrated and broken up. Terrifying sanctions were imposed on all dissenters, who had their tongues cut out or were burnt at the stake or hanged, measures which eventually brought about widespread revolts.

The Jesuits who had already introduced the murderous Inquisition as a prelude to their clerical colonialism, had hoped to easily overwhelm the opposition of the Ethiopian people. The Roman Catholic Patriarch had called the Ethiopian nobles together, and in the presence of the Emperor arrogantly ordered that they should kneel and swear allegiance to the patriarch as representative of the Pope. They further ordered that all priests of the Ethiopian Church be suspended until they could be re-ordained by him, and that the whole population be regarded as heathen unless they re-baptize under Jesuit supervision.

To these radical changes they added the introduction of graven images into the Ethiopian places of worship, which the Ethiopians regarded as idolatrous, and the abolition of circumcision. The majority of the Jesuit priests treated the Ethiopian religion as undiluted heresy, and in so doing, antagonized not only the clergy but also the ordinary public of Ethiopia.

The Ethiopians were unwilling to abandon their ancient faith, or to allow foreigners to treat with contempt the traditions and customs of their ancestors. They were further dismayed to learn that the Portuguese were seizing the best lands and the Jesuit clergy was rapidly assuming more than royal authority, procuring the elimination of all who opposed their purposes. General discontent became even more intense as the people of Ethiopia began to fully understand the catastrophic implications of the Jesuit intrigues. Revolt after revolt broke out, and as the civil war continued without any prospect of ending, the Emperor's loyal followers, including his own son Fasiladas, began to urge him to break with Rome, and his army began to murmur against having to fight against fellow Ethiopians.

61

The protests of the Ethiopian people against the imposition of the cult of Romanism in their millennarian Kingdom, swiftly evolved into a civil war. In the year 1621, in the province of Gojjam, Ras Seala Krestos, who was a prominent Roman Catholic, launched a devastating attack against a group of protestors and massacred the marching rebels which included a number of monks. Thereafter, armies were formed that marched against the King's forces. The confrontations developed into a large-scale fratricidal war between brothers, divided by the cunning devices of the subtle Jesuits who were bent on advancing the geopolitical ambitions of their master in Rome.

After defeating an opposing force of 25,000, Susenyos had the sorry duty of contemplating a battlefield littered with 8,000 dead, all of them his own subjects, his compatriots and fellow Ethiopians. In spite of the urgings of the Catholic Patriarch prodding Susenyos to defend the Latin faith to which he had pledged himself, the King refused to have any further bloodshed for the sake of a cause his people would rather die than submit to. So, on the 14th of June, 1632, Emperor Susenyos abdicated in favour of his son Fasiladas, who promptly reversed his father's religious policy, banishing the Jesuits from all Ethiopia.

And so ended the uprising against the Church of Rome in Ethiopia. The establishment of Rome's insidious form of religious despotism had cost the Ethiopian people much pain and suffering, but the pulling down of the elaborate structure that the Jesuits had laboriously built, required the effusion of much blood and the wasting of numerous lives.

In the vast slaughter and destruction experienced by the Ethiopians during the long years of war with Ahmed Gran and others, the majority of the monuments of Ethiopian antiquity were forever lost, and many hundreds of old Christian churches were burnt to the ground. Subsequently, a further period of anguish and material impoverishment came about with the religious civil war produced by the Portuguese attempt to impose the Roman doctrines and discipline.

When these tribulations were brought to a close with the expulsion of the Jesuits by the Emperor Fasiladas in 1632, the renowned genius of the Ethiopian people flowered anew during the period known among western historians as the Gondar era. Three successive reigns of considerable splendour in the great line of Solomonic kings, open this period. They were those of Emperors Fasiladas, Yohannes, and Iyasu the Great. Fasiladas (ruled 1632-1667) resolutely carried out the task of removing the catholic clergy from the country, and in order to prevent any further religious disturbances, the king barred all Europeans from entering the kingdom by any route. The most distinguished feature of his reign was the creation of a new capital at Gondar, north of Lake Tana. There he built the grandest and most magnificent of all the palaces that were to be constructed in that region, and for which Gondar is justly famous. So sturdy and strong is this Castle of Fasiladas, that it has withstood the earthquake of 1704, the civil wars which scourged Ethiopia in the eighteenth and nineteenth century, the pillage and burning by the host of the Mahdi of Sudan, and the bombardment of the British in 1941.

Yohannes (1667-1682), did not pursue his father's policy towards the Moslems, since he was becoming alarmed, early in his reign, at the expansion of Islam in the region. He had a liking for religious and philosophical learning, and especially for theological disputation which he avidly encouraged. These lively and extended debates were frequently held in the palace, where the more exuberant and impassioned participants had to sometimes be sent off to a more or less uninhabited island on Lake Tana, to meditate on the Scriptures.

A passage in the Royal Chronicles of Ethiopia, tells how on one occasion Yohannes had to rise swiftly from his throne in order to separate two of the scholars who had become somewhat overzealous in an argument over the meaning of a verse in the gospel of Matthew. His reign was also noted for a series of campaigns against the Agau people who inhabited the lands south of Lake Tana, during which their temples and idols were destroyed.

Upon the death of Emperor Yohannes, his son Iyasu the Great (1682-1706) ascended the throne and donned the Imperial mantle. He was the last great ruler of Ethiopia before the country fell into a period of some one hundred and fifty years of disorder and decay. His rulership was conducted on pious and orderly principles. A significant feature during this period, were the recurrent Synods where monks of different theological leanings discussed the nature of Christ, at times so vehemently as to bring forth a sharp rebuke from the King. The Royal Chronicles states that on the occasion of a visit to the Holy City of Aksum, he was the only person who was able to open the Sacred Ark of the Covenant, which none of the priests could unlock.

Iyasu had led a number of expeditions against the tribes of the Shankalla and also against the Galla. The latter were pagans and they had taken into slavery thousands of Christians who were periodically offered up as sacrifices to their Gods in celebration of battle victories. In these confrontations, Iyasu made virtual mincemeat of this tribe, and his soldiers threw down before him the head of their chief, and piled up mounds of their enemies prepuce which they slice from the uncircumcised, as they lay dead or dying upon the battlefield.

The reign of Iyasu was also marked by his love of magnificence and luxury. At Gondar he built a second palace which was claimed to be 'more beautiful than the palace of Solomon' and the Emperor was moved about in a carrying-chair of cedar that had posts of silver and a roof of gold, whilst he reclined therein upon heaps of purple cushions. The wealth and prosperity which characterized his reign was certainly due to the heavy caravan traffic between Ethiopia and the Eritrean ports.

In the end, however, Iyasu was forced to abdicate the throne in the face of his own son's insidious treachery, and he went into retreat on an island on Lake Tana. Yet, the plots and intrigues which were rampant within the court at Gondar, followed him there, and a few months later, when it was feared that he might return to the throne, assasins were sent in search of him and he was first shot, then killed by the sword. Iyasu the Great was regarded as a martyr and a saint, not only for the brutal manner of his death, but for his piety and love of justice.

With the murder of Iyasu the Great, there came upon the kingdom of Ethiopia a time of profound upheaval and disorder, at times bordering on open anarchy, punctuated by the frequent intrigues and machinations surrounding the Imperial throne. This period of considerable confusion was due, again, to the increasing influence of the Galla tribes in the capital, who were the source of much disturbance in political affairs.

The son of Iyasu the Great, Takla Haymanot, who had been responsible for the assassination of his father, was in turn murdered in 1708; and so, Theophilus, the brother of Iyasu assumed the Imperial titles and proceeded to avenge the royal murders, with the result that the Empress Malako-Tawit, who had prompted Takla Haymanot to put her own husband to death, was duly hanged. When Theophilus died in 1711 the throne was seized by Yostos, who was later poisoned by his enemies. He was followed in the line of succession to the throne by David III who only ruled long enough to build a 'Pavillion of Delight' next to the palace, before he too fell victim to the arts of the royal poisoners. During this period of marked instability, the Galla tribes invaded the capital at will, while the court remained largely preoccupied with theological controversies.

Emperor Bakuffa (1721-1750) who next ascended the throne, was much inclined to superstition and the interpretation of portents and omens. It had been prophesied that during the reign of his heir, a woman by the name of Walatta-Giyorgis would exercise supreme power, and so, for most of his reign Bakuffa pondered deeply upon the ways and means of dealing with this mysterious usurper-to-be. On one occasion, the Emperor journeyed incognito to Kuara, a district west of Lake Tana, which was a notoriously unhealthy area, where he developed a sudden illness. In the salubrious climate of the adjoining highlands, there lived a man of distinction who was also very charitable. And upon learning of the unfortunate stranger, had him carried up to his own residence, where he was nursed by his host's lovely daughter, Berhan Magass (Glory of Grace), after which the Emperor quickly recovered.

Upon returning to his throne he sent for the beautiful damsel who had tended him, and made her his Empress. Apart from her great beauty, she was also possessed with a sweet and generous disposition, as well as exceptional intelligence and discretion. They had a son, the future Iyasu II, while Berhan Magass was later given the throne name Mentuab, meaning 'How beautiful thou art'. One day Emperor Bakuffa told Mentuab the story of the prophecy, which he had never before mentioned, and was greatly relieved to learn from her that the name Walatta-Giyorgis was her baptismal name. This reassured him that on his death, the Empress would become Regent to the throne, during the period of their son's minority.

With the death of Bakuffa, his son Iyasu II ascended the throne while still a child, and Mentuab did indeed rule as Regent during the minority of her son and subsequently of her grandson, retaining her influence in state affairs for almost three decades. Her renowned beauty remained with her even in her mature years. It seems she had Portuguese blood, and did show a marked leaning towards Roman Catholicism, possibly for that reason. Iyasu II did enjoy sufficient authority which his mother had endeavored to secure for him from trusted allies, and he was thus able to put down the many uprisings and disturbances instigated by rival pretenders to the throne.

Iyasu II died at a young age, leaving an empire that was torn asunder by deep political conflicts. The new king was his half-brother Yoas who was still a minor, and who was proclaimed even before the death of his predecessor. Yoas was the son of Iyasu's Gala wife, a fact which greatly encouraged the Wollo tribes, who were progressively granted more and more concessions, while at the same time they sought to retain their independence. There began then a period of decadence which anticipated and pointed to the eventual decline and final fall of the great Ethiopian capital of Gondar, and it appeared as if the legendary Dynasty of the Blessed Seed was doomed to end in a quiet eclipse.

A series of puppet kings who were entirely at the mercy of ambitious nobles, dominated this post-Gondarine period of modern Ethiopian history. Among the most powerful and influential, was Ras Mikael, a Tigrean Prince and warlord who had cleverly arranged for himself and his sons, marriage with the daughters of Empress Mentuab. On the occasion of an attack on Ras Mikael by one of the royal servants, which he narrowly escaped, revenge was taken by his cohorts, and Emperor Yoas was strangled in his palace. Ras Mikael then sent for the younger brother of Iyasu II, who was then at the Wahni, a prison where the rival claimants to the throne are kept; but this brother who was then 70 years of age, died just a few months after being enthroned. He was replaced by his son Takla Haymanot II, a courageous, energetic and remarkably patient man.

The internecine wars that constantly erupted as rebels and various malcontents vied for positions of power, frequently came very close to the Imperial court. One of the retaliatory attacks of the opposing Galla tribe led by Ras Gusho, who had defeated the powerful Ras Mikael, was launched against the Emperor in revenge for the murder of Yoas, and in 1779 the Galla forces invaded the palace and massacred the king while he was sleeping. He was succeeded on the throne by his brother Takla Giyorgis who reigned sporadically until 1800, when the clashes between various provincial chiefs became so intense that he was compelled to seek refuge among the hermits of the Woldebba region.

The kingdom at this time was beginning to fragment into a series of largely independent states; Tigre, Lasta, Gojjam, Begameder, and Shoa. It was in the midst of these profound regional divisions and constant strife that frequently ravaged the nation, that there emerged on the scene a Prince of the Solomonic line, who was destined to be a major force in restoring unity to the Imperial realm. Prince Kasa of Kuara was born in 1821, at a time when the ambitious Mehemet Ali was embarking on a campaign to expand Egypt into the Sudan, thereby threatening Ethiopia's northern borders. Later on, he led several successful assaults on the enemy forces, and by skilful diplomacy had gotten France and England to intervene in order to compel Mehemet Ali to reverse his whole campaign against Ethiopia.

Kasa had succeeded in bringing about the unity of Ethiopia

after a long break of over one hundred years, and under the influence of an ancient prophecy of the *Fekare-Iyesus* which stated that a ruler named Theodore would arise and extend his empire as far as Jerusalem. Kasa was crowned emperor on the 5th of May 1855 and was given the throne name Theodore II, after which he proclaimed himself as the Emperor named in the prophecies, who would arise to deliver the kingdom and unify her dominions.

Under his rule, significant judicial and administrative reforms were instituted, and continuous and highly effective campaigns were carried out against the ever-ambitious nobles, and invaders such as the Gallas, the Yeju and the encroaching Moslems. In order to make a total break with the court at Gondar, Theodore transferred his capital to Makdala in the province of Amhara, in the process removing all the remaining wealth from the former capital and stripping the treasure of forty-four churches, including some 900 precious manuscripts which were all taken to the new seat of government.

The extraordinary propensity for violence exhibited by Emperor Theodore became a dark blot on his reign. Apart from the constant persecution of clergy and laity, a veritable flood of murders kept the population in a state of mass terror and perpetual trepidation. A single word, or even an ill-conceived gesture, could lead to the death of it's author. Quarrels of all sorts with priests and clerics went on incessantly, and during the repression of peasants, it was common to have whole villages burnt down while the inhabitants were shut in their houses.

In his campaigns against the Turks and other Moslem tribes that were constantly pressing against Ethiopia's northern frontiers, Theodore thought that Britain as a Christian power, would come to his aid, and accordingly, in 1862 he wrote a letter to Queen Victoria proposing a comprehensive alliance. Britain however, had just concluded a treaty with Turkey against Russia, and the Foreign Office was in no hurry to respond to Theodore's proposals. The protracted two year silence which greeted his message, deeply offended the Emperor who forthwith imprisoned the British Consul and a number of other Europeans.

When all diplomatic efforts failed to secure the release of the foreign prisoners, a military expeditionary force under Sir Robert Napier landed in Ethiopia in December 1867, and on the 13th of April 1868 with the fall of Makdala, Emperor Theodore committed suicide in order to avoid capture. The entire library of manuscripts, and all the vast wealth and treasures that were at the palace were taken away by the British soldiers, to be subsequently disseminated to museums, universities and private collections in Britain and throughout Europe, where they remain to this day. Despite the tragic sequence of events which ended the turbulent reign of Theodore, his struggle for Ethiopian liberty and unity to abolish feudal separatism bore fruit in later times.

The death of Theodore was followed by four years of constant intrigues and bickering, until at length Johannes IV (1872-1889) was crowned at Aksum. The province of Shoa did not come under his jurisdiction, for Menyelek (II) the able son of the Shoan ruler Haile Malakot, had taken over his father's throne. Johannes however, was almost immediately faced with important political anxieties of an unprecedented kind, for the empire, which had suddenly emerged from a state of lengthy isolation, found itself surrounded by the threatening forces of the major European powers, exhibiting great interest in the Red Sea coastal regions and the lands of the Upper Nile.

Emperor Johannes IV had to confront major war waged by the Khedive Ismail. The opening of the Suez Canal in 1869 had enhanced predatory ambitions in the Red Sea area. The almost impregnable fortress of Keren was betrayed by the Swiss adventurer Werner Munzinger, who had married a daughter of one of the local families and had succeeded in winning the confidence of the neighbouring people. Though the Egyptians were fully equipped with the latest modern arms of the period and were trained and led by American and European officers, their forces were forcefully repelled, and in 1875 Munzinger's army and that of Arakel Bey were hacked to pieces by Johannes on the Mareb river.

Ethiopian courage and tenacity in defence of the homeland

succeeded in repelling the foreign invaders, despite their great superiority in arms. These victories against tremendous odds evoked the enthusiasm of the nation. Nevertheless, the war had created great havoc; the enemy had ravaged as far as Asmara; crops and vegetation had been destroyed over an extensive area, and Keren was still under Egyptian occupation. Later, in 1887, a *Dervish* host smashed their way through the troops of the *Negus* of Gojjam and poured into Gondar, sacking and burning the city and massacring its inhabitants. Emperor Johannes retaliated a year later by slaughtering over 60,000 followers of the Mahdi at Matamma, but he was wounded in the battle and died shortly after. In the course of his reign he had indicated his hatred of Catholics, Moslems and pagans by making conversion of the infidels a compulsory measure in 1878. Religious liberty in the realm was not restored until after his death.

The Solomonic Dynasty of Israel Kings continued in Ethiopia with the proclamation and crowning of Menyelek II (1889-1913), a truly extraordinary figure in the annals of Ethiopia's modern history, who within some twenty years succeeded in transforming and enlarging the legendary mountain kingdom in a most remarkable way, pushing forward his frontiers to Gedaref, Khartoum and Lake Victoria. The first major problem he had to confront, however, was the Italian infiltration which was taking place in the north.

Italy had purchased the port of Asab in 1882 from a private trading company and formed a colony there. Then, in 1885 the Italians landed at Massaua while the British took Zaila and Berbera, and the French occupied Djibuti. Menyelek had come to an initial agreement recognizing Italian sovereignty north of the Mareb river, and linked his foreign policy to that of Italy by signing the infamous Treaty of Uccialli in May 1889.

A disagreement in respect of the translated versions of the treaty, however, forced Menyelek to renounce the treaty.

The Ethiopians looked with increasing misgivings upon the advance of the Italians, who by 1894 had reached as far as the region of Adwa and Enda-Mohoni. Later on, in September of that year, the Emperor ordered a mass conscription of all able bodied males, and he set out for the north to meet the enemy.

The difficulties with the Treaty of Uccialli began when the Italian Prime Minister, Francesco Crispi, interpreted the ambiguous Article 17 as implying the declaration of an Italian protectorate over Ethiopia, on the basis of which Italy proceeded to coin money with the impress of the Italian king Umberto I, wearing the Ethiopian crown; furthermore, the Italian possessions in Africa were constituted as "Colonia Eritrea". After the repudiation of the Treaty altogether, Menyelek prepared to combat the Italians' attempt to impose their dominion militarily.

Italian victories at the beginning of the campaign were brilliant but fruitless, and at the end of 1895 massive Ethiopian armies were threatening Italian outposts. The Italian governor of Eritrea, General Oreste Baratieri, sighted Menyelek's forces on the 7th of February 1896, but remained inactive while the Ethiopians withdrew to Adwa. Goaded by furious telegraphic communications from Rome, Baratieri desperately tried to save face and protect his reputation, and advanced to Adwa with a force of 20,000 disorganized, mismanaged and ill-equipped men, against Menyelek's army of over 80,000.

The presence in the battlefield of the courageous Emperor Menyelek and his consort, the celebrated warrior-queen Empress Taitu with her corps of female attendants and nurses, greatly inspired the Ethiopian defenders. On the first of March 1896 the Imperial army was attacked in the Adwa mountains by the Italian forces under General Baratieri. The ensuing epic battle which lasted only two days, marked the last occasion when the Sacred Ark of the Covenant was brought out of its resting place, to lead, as in the days of Old Testament Israel, God's people in confrontation with their enemies. The Italian army was swiftly and humiliatingly routed, and their troops cut to pieces, in a decisive victory for the Ethiopians who pursued the retreating remnants through difficult mountainous terrain, while a hostile population joined in harassing the fleeing invaders.

The Italian invasion of the time was the first instance on which the independence and integrity of Ethiopia had been menaced since the wars of the sixteenth century promoted by Turkey. The battle of Adwa was the culmination of a premeditated attempt to conquer and subjugate the country, which was completely frustrated by the disastrous defeat of the Italian armies.

Ethiopia's international prestige soared to great heights as news of the victory spread throughout the world, while numerous chronicles in the metropolitan press sang the praises of the remote and exotic ancient kingdom in Africa, led by a black king and his mysterious and beautiful warrior-queen, which inflicted such devastating blows on the forces of a major European power.

At the same time, in Italy, major riots broke out in the capital city of Rome, and in Milan, Venice and Florence, where angry throngs of weeping mothers demanded from the government the return of their sons who were sent to die an inglorious death upon African soil. The ensuing crisis brought down the government of Prime Minister Crispi shortly after, ending for a time at least, Italy's colonial ambitions in Africa. Menyelek insisted that there should be no acts of revenge against the defeated Italians, allowing all the prisoners of war to be repatriated but only after walking through a body of shallow water, so that they 'should not take back with them even the dust from the Ethiopian soil.'

Ethiopia had nevertheless sustained great losses and her suffering as a result of the Italian invasion was not insignificant. From the region of Adwa itself, terrible accounts of the famine and cholera that had devastated the country, started to emerge; the locusts also had destroyed almost all the crops and cattle, disease broke out and killed most of the horned cattle. The population began to starve and a malignant sort of typhus fever broke out, decimating whole families, with even entire villages perishing. A burying party of Italian army engineers had been allowed by the government to come and inter the dead, but the condition of the corpses prevented them from being moved, so they were only covered with loose stones.

Eyewitnesses accounts shortly after the end of the battle showed what the country had gone through; the majority of the houses were unroofed and broken down; skulls of men and bones of animals were strewn all around, and the remains of unburied humanity issued forth the sickly smell of decaying flesh, which could be scented from miles away. The nation however, as it had many times before, drew strength from the fountain of its deep spirituality, to go forward into a promising future of progress, peace and unity, the ever-present tenets of her lofty ideals.

Under the wise leadership of Emperor Menyelek II, Ethiopia now embarked on a major modernisation program with the help of foreign technicians. Previously in 1893, the Emperor had founded Addis Ababa "New Flower" as his capital city and new governmental centre. When his cousin Ras Makonnen died in 1907, Menyelek wept for three days for his greatest and ablest official, who for so many years had been his right-hand man and confidant. As the Emperor was advancing in age he nominated as his successor his grandson Lij Eyasu, who was still a child. Lij Eyasu was the son of Ras Mikael of Worra Himano. Later, in 1911, Ras Tasama was appointed Regent until the death of Menyelek in 1913.

Lij Eyasu however, was widely detested from the moment that he was made Emperor, both, on account of his evident incompetence as well as his Moslem leanings. Consequently, a powerful coalition of the princes of Shoa exercised their considerable influence to have him deposed by the *Abuna* who nominated the daughter of Menyelek, Zauditu, as Empress, with Ras Tafari, the son of the great Ras Makonnen, as Regent and heir to the throne. Lij Eyasu's father, Ras Mikael, tried in vain to prevent the downfall of his son by force of arms, but was eventually defeated and Lij Eyasu fled in the face of the daunting opposition that confronted him.

When Menyelek's daughter, Zauditu, became Empress of Ethiopia in 1917, the Regency and real power behind the throne was exercised by Ras Tafari Makonnen, whose powerful personality was destined to eclipse the vacillating and weak Empress, and by 1928 when he acquired the title of *Negus*, he had clearly become the dominant power. Ras Tafari Makonnen was a great-grandson of Sahle Selassie of Shoa and a son of Ras Makonnen, chief adviser to Emperor Menyelek II. When the Empress died in 1930, he assumed full authority as Emperor, taking the name Haile Selassie (Might of the Trinity) and the inherited Solomonic titles: King of Kings, Lord of Lords, Conquering Lion of the Tribe of Judah, Elect of God, Light of the Universe. He is undoubtedly the greatest king in the modern history of Ethiopia.

The resplendent pomp and pageantry that attended the coronation of the Emperor Haile Selassie I and his royal consort the Empress Menem, rubricated the profound significance that the advent of this last King of the legendary Solomonic dynasty represented for Ethiopia and the world. The magnificent event which was witnessed by royalty and state dignitaries from around the world, saw the representative of the British Crown, the Duke of Gloucester, returning the 'Scepter of Righteousness' to the new Ethiopian King. The richly ornate and jeweled royal scepter had been taken away to Britain during the Napier military invasion of 1868.

Ras Tafari Makonnen was born on the 23rd of July, 1892 near Harer. He was the ninth pregnancy of his mother, Waizero Yeshibamet who died in childbirth, he being the only one of her children to survive beyond infancy. While still in his teens he was appointed governor of Sidamo and then of Harer, during which time he began instituting progressive policies, seeking to break the feudal power of the local nobility, by increasing the authority of the central government. In 1931 a new constitution was promulgated which recognized his exalted ancestry and the unique qualities that were personified in him.

The Ethiopian constitution established in its 2nd article the principles upon which the Monarch's Divine Right to Rule is based, categorically stating, thus:

"The Imperial dignity shall remain perpetually attached to the line of Haile Selassie I, whose line descends without interruption from the dynasty of Menyelek I, son of the Queen of Ethiopia, the Queen of Sheba and King Solomon of Jerusalem.

By virtue of His Imperial Blood, as well as by the anointing which He has received, the Person of the Emperor is sacred, His dignity inviolable and His power indisputable."

And indeed, Emperor Haile Selassie I was in fact the Ethiopian Government, and the destiny of the kingdom rested entirely upon his personal vision and wise leadership. His prestige and international stature were fully recognized throughout the world, and in his many official visits to foreign countries, the inevitable aura of mysticism and the fascinating, legendary origins of his millenarian mountain kingdom always shone forth in the enigmatic and mysterious personality of the 'Lion of Judah'.

It was in the Western Hemisphere, however, that the Messianic, Israelite features of the Solomonic dynasty of Kings in Ethiopia were fully outlined and given cogent expression, with the emergence of the prophetic movement of the Rastafarians. Appearing in the early 1930's, among the most downtrodden sectors of African slave descendants, in the teeming slums of Jamaica's capital city of Kingston; the early Rastafarian pioneers were inspired by the prophetic utterances of the great black leader Marcus Garvey, who anticipated a redemption for all Africans, with the impending crowning of a promised 'Black King' in the African motherland. The coronation of the *Negus* Ras Tafari in Ethiopia was seen as the fulfillment of this prophecy.

Haile Selassie I, last monarch to sit on the Throne of David in Ethiopia, is recognized as the 'Seal of the Dynasty' because so many of the messianic promises in the Holy Scriptures were fulfilled in his person.

An analysis of the prophetic fulfillment and comparison of

Haile Selassie I and Jesus Christ, manifestly showed numerous parallelisms which cannot be easily thrown aside. For, when in Matthew 24: 3, 29, Christ's apostles asked him, "What shall be the sign of thy coming?" Christ said, "Immediately after the tribulation of those days shall the sun be darkened, and the moon shall not give her light, and the stars shall fall from heaven, and the powers of the heavens shall be shaken...So likewise ye, when ye shall see all these things, know that it is near, even at the doors." (Matt. 24: 33) The 19th of May, 1780, is known in history as the 'Dark Day' because an unexplained darkness on this day covered a large portion of the New World. Thus the sun was darkened and the moon did not give any light on the night following this 'Dark Day'. Then, on the 13th of November 1833, the stars of the heavens all fell in a shower across the firmament, fulfilling another of the Saviour's prophecies of the nearness of his coming.

Christ had said in Luke 24:44, "...all things must be fulfilled, which were written in the law of Moses, and in the prophets, and in the psalms, concerning me." And in Psalm 68:31 it says, "Ethiopia shall soon stretch out her hands to God." Then, in Psalm 87:4 the Lord said, "...behold Philistia, and Tyre, with Ethiopia; this man was born there."

Analyzing this sentence: *This man* was born there. The subject of the sentence is *this man*. The subject of the Psalm is *the Lord*. *The Lord* is the noun of the Psalm and *this man* is the pronoun. But, a pronoun is used instead of a noun, and a pronoun must follow a noun. Therefore, by substitution, *This man* was born there = *The Lord* was born there. *There* is the object in this sentence and is functioning as a demonstrative pronoun of place. The grammatical logic to determine whether the object "there" refers either to Philistia, Tyre or Ethiopia is revealed by the preposition, *with*. The preposition *with*, dictates that Ethiopia is the noun for the demonstrative object pronoun, *there*. Therefore, this sentence, "*This man* was born there" = *The Lord* was born in Ethiopia. Again, we substituted *there* for Ethiopia.

Christ was born in Bethlehem of Judah *in His first advent*; therefore, according to Psalm 87:4, 'The Lord was born in Ethio-

76

pia' must be fulfilled in Christ's second coming. On the 23d of July, 1892 Haile Selassie I was born in Ethiopia. The stars fell shortly before on the 13th of November 1833 and on the 19th of May 1780 the sun and the moon were darkened. Prophesied signs of His coming. Hebrews 7:14 states, "For it is evident that our Lord sprang out of Judah," Haile Selassie I is a direct descendant from the union of King Solomon and the Queen of Sheba. He is from the tribe of Judah.

Further, in Revelation 22:16, Christ said, "I am the root and the offspring of David." Again, Haile Selassie I is an offspring of David. Then in Revelation 1:14-15 "His head and His hairs were white like wool". Only black people have wooly (sheep-like hair, locks). Christ was a Nazarite and had locks. Haile Selassie I also had wooly hair… "and his feet like unto fine brass, as if they burned in a furnace." Brass is the color of black people's skin and when brass is burned it gets even blacker. Christ was a black man, He being of the tribe of Judah, as Haile Selassie is also a black man.

Among the many prophecies that foretold the return of Christ *in the flesh* to manifest His kingly character according to the Davidic Covenant (II Samuel 7:4-5, 12-16), the statement in I John 4:2-3 emphatically states, "Every spirit that confesseth that Jesus Christ is come in the flesh is of God… and every spirit that confesseth not that Jesus Christ is come in the flesh is not of God". Therefore, expect the Christ anytime *in the flesh* after the 13th of November, 1833, because the falling of the stars fulfilled the prophecy which pertains to the nearness of Christ's coming.

This is further emphasized in Acts 2:29-30. Peter said, "…let me freely speak unto you of the patriarch David,…Therefore, being a prophet, and knowing that God had sworn with an oath to him, that of the fruit of his loins, *according to the flesh*, he would raise up Christ to sit on his throne." But Christ did not sit on King David's throne *during his first advent*; yet, this prophecy must be fulfilled, as Christ himself said that all prophecies about himself must be fulfilled (Luke 24:44). Haile Selassie I did sit on King David's throne and, thus, fulfilled the prophecy in Acts

77

2:29-30, because he is the fruit of King David's loins according to the flesh, being the direct descendant from David's son King Solomon and the Queen of Sheba.

At his coronation in November 1930, Haile Selassie I was prophetically anointed with the Biblical titles: King of Kings and Lord of Lords (Revelation 19:16), The Lion of the Tribe of Judah (Revelation 5:5, Psalm 99:3); and most evidently, he also fulfilled I Timothy 6:15, "Which in his times he shall shew, who is the blessed and only Potentate, the King of kings, and Lord of lords;" dwelling upon the earth during his monarchical reign.

When this prophetically anointed king of the Royal House of David was born, Ethiopia was experiencing a protracted drought lasting several months, parching the land which was thereafter denuded of a large portion of its vegetation. Haile Selassie's birth was welcomed at that very moment with widespread lightning and peals of thunder followed by a considerable downpour of water. Many in the remote province of Harer, learnt of the birth of Ras Makonnen's son many weeks and even many months after; but, upon ascertaining the time of his arrival, realized that the welcome rains heralded the advent of a man-child marked by destiny, who would certainly bring forth once more, the longed-for greatness, glory and dignity, that was in previous times the natural heritage of their ancient and mystical land.

Ras Tafari Makonnen was brought up according to the Royal Custom and tradition due to a person of his stature, with strict royal discipline; he was also cultivated in Ethiopian religious moral values unique to his heritage, with a balanced mixture of academic, military and spiritual guidance.

When in early 1935, Italy, under the fascist dictatorship of Benito Mussolini issued threatening remarks regarding their increasing ambitions to expand their control of Eritrea to the whole of Ethiopia, the leading nations of the world did nothing to stop an impending and unwarranted aggression. The international community thought that allowing the fascists to expand Italy's sphere of influence in Africa, would appease the ravenous appetite of the "axis powers" Germany and Italy, who were acting on full accord, joined as they were by their so-called 'Pact of Steel'. By sacrificing Ethiopia to the nazi-fascist alliance, Europe was hoping to keep the flames of war away from their home territory, as well as safeguarding their own colonial interests in the rest of Africa.

And the Roman aggression against the kingdom of Ethiopia was prophesied by the visionary Daniel, many centuries ago: "And *at the time of the end* shall the king of the south push at him; and the king of the north shall come against him like a whirlwind, with chariots, and with horsemen, and with many ships; and he shall enter into the countries, and shall overflow and pass over." (Daniel 11:40).

The king of the north is the emperor of the Roman Empire in ecclesiatical garb, the Pope; and the king of the south can only be Ethiopia, the only country in all East Africa that continued independent, and had a government and kingdom dating back before the Roman Empire. At the time of the end, this king of the south, Ethiopia, was to push at the king of the north, Rome. In March 1896, Italy had suffered a crushing defeat to Ethiopian forces under King Menyelek II at the Battle of Adwa, as the Italians were cut to pieces because of their inexperience in fighting in mountainous country, and because they were greatly outnumbered. This defeat was disastrous to Italian expansionist ambitions in Africa.

Ever since, Italy demanded revenge. In 1927 Mussolini set the time, at just under 40 years from that defeat, or 1935, when he would be ready... "finally to make our voice heard, and see our rights recognized!" And that fateful year 1935 came when Mussolini attacked, "like a whirlwind" he did send a great air force into Africa, also many modern "chariots" – trucks, tanks, armoured vehicles, etc. – and ships, loaded with soldiers. More than 100,000 sailed to Ethiopia.

Emboldened by the impotence and spineless attitude of the League of Nations, who failed to protect its weaker members from unprovoked attack, Italy invaded Ethiopia, unleashing against her the destructive might of their demolishing war machine. In the tradition of the warrior-emperor, Haile Selassie personally led the resistance against the invaders, no longer bringing forth the Holy Ark of the Covenant to battle, for He himself knew that He was the personification of the Holy Ark, prophetically destined to lead his people, as in the days of old, David had led Israel in its wars against the Amorites.

The anguish and disaster that overtook Ethiopia during the fascist invasion was truly a bitter ordeal for its king, who resolutely led the determined resistance to the foreign aggression. There he was in the midst of heated battles, seated on the white horse '*that pawed in the valley of Armageddon and disturbed the waters of the seven seas, from Gibraltar even unto Mandalay;*' and the fires of that epic conflagration did spread to engulf all nations, for Italy's attack against the kingdom of Ethiopia marked the beginning of the second world war.

After much persuasion from family members and from Ethiopian officials, in May 1936 Emperor Haile Selassie went into exile in Britain. On the last day of June, 1936, in the Swiss city of Geneva, the delegates of fifty-two countries gathered in the vast assembly hall of the League of Nations, where almost every civilized country in the world was represented. The press galleries were filled with reporters. The League of Nations, founded after World War I, was being put to the test by a remote and half-forgotten country whose very existence was being snuffed out by the guns and the bombs of Italian Fascist troopers. The honour of the civilized world was at stake.

There was almost total silence in the great hall, as a slim, bearded, dark-faced figure was escorted to the speaker's platform. He was dressed in white, with a black cape over his shoulders, and his face was calm. There was about him an inescapable sense of Majesty. He was a king and he looked like a king. His bearing was regal, almost austere, and his dignity brought the delegates to their feet as a mark of respect. Haile Selassie I, Emperor of

cont'd. on page 98

80

Pictorial, Maps
and Drawings

Ethiopian traditional style painting depicting the visit of the Queen of Sheba to King Solomon at Jerusalem.

(Courtesy, Atsede Mariam, E.O.C.)

David, Son of Jesse and father of Solomon (1 Samuel 16:11-13)

(Courtesy, Dr. Malachi York)

Solomon, Son of David and Bathsheba. (II Samuel 5:14)
(Courtesy, Dr. Malachi York)

83

Joseph, Stepfather of Iyesus (Jesus) Kristos. (Matthew 1:16)
(Courtesy, Dr. Malachi Z. York)

Mary, Mother of Iyesus Kristos (Jesus). (Matthew 1:16)
(Courtesy, Dr. Malachi Z. York)

The Holy Family flight to Egypt-Ethiopia. Traditional sacred iconography taken from Makdala by British soldiers during the Napier invasion of 1868. Now resting at the British Museum, London.

(Courtesy Atsede Mariam, E.O.C.)

'King of Kings' Menyelek II and the African 'Warrior Queen' Empress Taitu. They inflicted a crushing defeat on invading Italian armies at the Battle of Adwa in Ethiopia (1896).

(Courtesy, Atsede Mariam, E.O.C.)

In action during the Italo-Abyssinian War (1936). The Ethiopian King Haile Selassie I, manning his Oerlikon anti-aircraft gun. He personally led the Ethiopian forces in the war against the Italian agressors under Mussolini's fascist regime.

(Courtesy, Haile Mikael, E.W.F.)

The Negus, Haile Selassie I

The coronation of the Emperor of Ethiopia, formerly the Prince Ras Tafari, at
Addis Ababa, the Abyssinian Capital, on November 2, 1930. He is shown
wearing the crown and carrying the sceptre and the orb, amid scenes of great
magnificence.

(Courtesy, Ras Ivi Tafari, Nyahbinghi Order, Jamaica)

86

The Empress of Ethiopia

Waizeru Menem, Ras Tafari's wife, also crowned as Empress of Ethiopia on November 2, 1930. The Queen Omega on her throne beneath a red canopy, gold-fringed and richly brocaded, reveals the unmistakable aura of majesty and royal dignity.

(Photo courtesy of Ras Ivi Tafari, Nyahbinghi Order, Jamaica)

Sanctuary of the Ark. Church of Saint Mary of Zion in the holy city of Aksum, Ethiopia. The Ark of the Covenant rests in seclusion at an underground compartment next to the sanctuary.

(Photo, courtesy of Atsede Mariam, E.O.C.)

Ashantiland Warrior, Defender of the Realm.
Artistic conception by A.G.C. Davy 'Birdlegs'

"Lion of Judah"

The Church pays homage to the Negus H.I.M. Haile Selassie I, Emperor of Ethiopia, Elect of God, Light of the Universe.

(Courtesy of Ras Ivi Tafari, Nyahbinghi Order, Jamaica)

"King of Kings"

H.I.M. His Imperial Majesty Haile Selassie I, "Behold, the Lion of the tribe of Judah, the Root of David, hath prevailed to open the book..."

Revelation 5:5

(Courtesy, Ivi Tafari, Nyahbinghi Order, Jamaica)

H.I.H. Prince, Ermias Sahle
Selassie, Chairman of the
Crown Council of Ethiopia,
Grandson of H.I.M. Haile
Selassie I. Carrier of the
"Blessed Seed".

*(Photo, Courtesy Sis.
Arianne Giraud)*

The Viceroy of Ethiopia, H.I.H.
Prince, Bekere Fikre Selassie, Great-
grandson of H.I.M. Haile Selassie.
Carrier of the "Blessed Seed".

(Courtesy, Reginald Trelford)

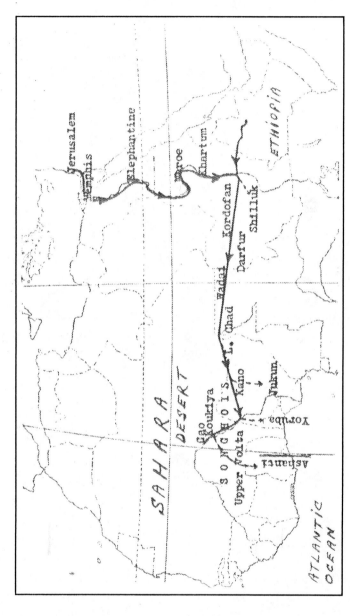

Course of migration of ancient Hebrew-Jewish priesthood (of the African Judah) from the Nile river valley to the Niger river area of Ashantiland. Royal Ashanti-Koromantyn caste arrives in Jamaica on the slave ships, to emerge centuries later as the prophetic movement of Ras Tafari. (Maps by Joseph Williams, SJ; From Nile to Niger).

92

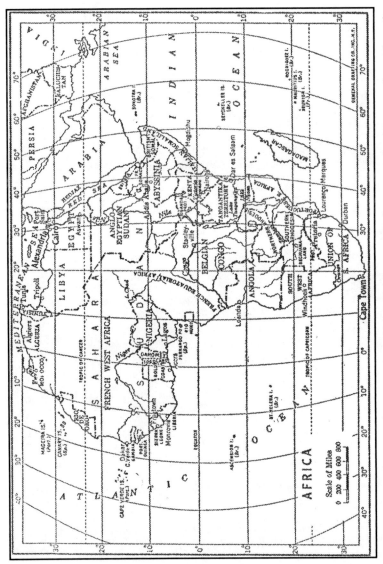

Africa in the 1920's. Hemmed in by the European powers who have carved out among themselves the 'Land of the Blacks' imposing Colonial borders across ancient Kingdoms and tribal domains.

Ashanti-Koromantyn ambassadors crossing the Pra River during the Ashanti-British wars of the 1820's. Notice the twelve-division breastplate of Ashanti official; it is identical to the one carried by ancient Jewish High Priest in Jerusalem. *(Drawing by Henry Morton, Courtesy, Fr. G. McLaughlin, SJ).*

94

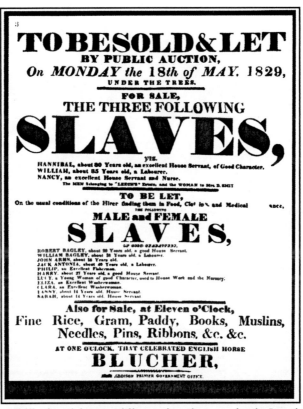

Handbill advertising a public auction slave market in Jamaica.

(Courtesy of Johnette Simmons, Nyahbinghi Order, Jamaica).

Slave auction in Virginia, USA, in the 1840's after Emancipation had been declared in Jamaica.

Slaves on embarkation canoe, going from coast to large slave ship off West Africa..

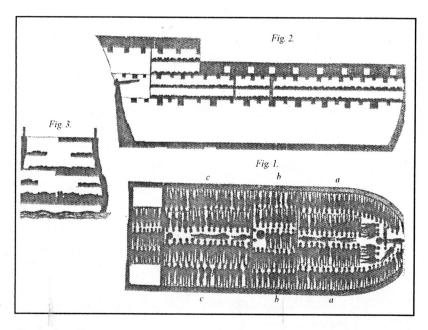

Illustration showing how the slaves were packed in an 18th century British slave ship for the transatlantic voyage, the Middle Passage, to the West Indies.

(Courtesy, Johnette Simmons).

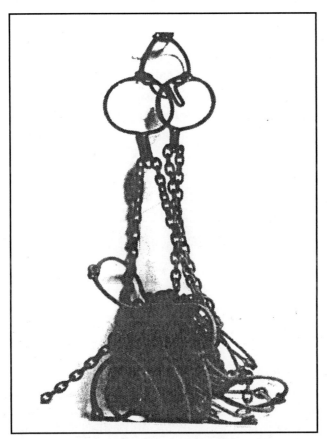

English-made chains and manacles used in African slave trade.

(From J. Simmons, Nyahbinghi Order, Jamaica)

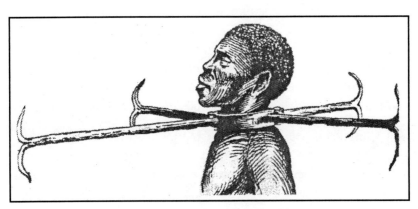

Iron slave-yoke on a captured African.

Ethiopia, King of Kings, Conquering Lion of the Tribe of Judah, had come to the court of international justice to plead for the very life of his country. And thus was fulfilled the utterance of the prophet Joel (3:2) "I will also gather all nations, and will bring them down into the valley of Jehoshaphat, and will plead with them there for my people and for my heritage Israel, whom they have scattered among the nations, and parted my land."

From the press gallery, Italian journalists shouted insults and obscenities at the tragic and lonely figure on the rostrum. They were removed by the guards and order was restored. In a low voice, using his native Amharic language, the Emperor spoke:

"I, Haile Selassie I, Emperor of Ethiopia, am here today to claim that justice is due to my people." He told the delegates how the Italian armies had invaded his country in violation of all international treaties. He told of the terror that had rained from the skies, for the fascist pilots (one of them was the son of Mussolini himself) had used poison gas as well as bombs.

"Men and animals succumbed. The deadly rain that fell from the aircraft made all those whom it touched flee, shrieking with intense pain. All who drank the poisoned water or ate the contaminated food perished too, in dreadful suffering. In tens of thousands, the victims of the Italian mustard gas died. It was to denounce to the civilized world the tortures inflicted upon the Ethiopian people, that I resolved to come to Geneva ..."

When the Emperor spoke at Geneva more than a generation ago, only his country had suffered the full force of terror from the skies. What had happened in Ethiopia was a rehearsal of things to come. In his quiet voice, the dark-faced monarch was giving the delegates at Geneva a forecast of what would happen if the world now chose to ignore the brutal invasion of his country.

"Apart from the Kingdom of God," he said, "no nation on this earth is superior to any other. If a strong government can destroy a weak people, then the hour has struck for all weak peoples. I appeal to the League of Nations to give it's judgment in all freedom. God and history will remember your decision..."

When the Emperor finished, there were tears in the eyes of some of the delegates, and the representatives of small nations shuddered with fear for their own future. But the great free nations of the world were afraid, and they merely mumbled pious regrets, since they believed that they could buy peace and safety from Mussolini, if only they allowed him to take Ethiopia.

As the ineffable and majestic King was leaving the great League of Nations assembly hall in Geneva, to begin a long and bitter exile in England, he issued forth the prophetic words that would shortly after be fulfilled as a terrible judgement upon the modern Gentile nations: "Today it is us, tomorrow it will be you."

Many years were to pass and all the world was to be scorched by war before the solemn and resilient Emperor was again to set foot in his own country. While in exile, Haile Selassie suffered insults and disappointments, for he had lost the right to rule his country, as well as much of the prestige he had enjoyed. But three things he never lost. These were his pride, his courage, and his faith. For he was a Christian king of the ancient dynastic line of the Royal House of David and Solomon, and a deep sense of destiny burned within him. He was content to wait on the judgement of God, while he drew strength from the millenarian line of kings who had for so many centuries – two thousand years and more – maintained the independence of their strange and mysterious mountain kingdom.

In Rome, when Mussolini's armies were preparing to leave for their so-called 'civilizing mission' in Ethiopia, the reigning ecclesiastical Ceasar, Pope Pius XI, gave his blessings to the expeditionary forces, the modern gladiators going forth on their terrible mission against a people who had done their nation no wrong, while his clerics were likewise blessing the tanks, guns and bombs that would wreak their havoc among defenceless African men, women and children.

Ethiopia sustained an unprovoked and unwarranted Italian invasion carried out by Italian troops in great numbers and enjoying an immense superiority in arms of every description. Despite the protests and condemnation of the civilized world, the invaders employed poison gas as well as incendiary and high-explosive bombs, indiscriminately machine-gunning the common people, and spraying vast areas of the country, towns, villages, farms and lakes with poison gas.

The fascist warplanes did their murderous work unhindered, for Ethiopia possessed neither military aeroplanes nor antiaircraft guns. It was, however, the poison gas, sprayed as a deadly dew, destroying the eyes, burning through the clothing and the flesh to the very bones, which had the most devastating effect. The hideous invasion was described by an eyewitness in these moving terms: "This isn't a war- it isn't even a slaughter-it's the torture of tens of thousands of defenceless men, women and children, with bombs and poison gas. They're using gas incessantly, brutally maiming and permanently scarring even infants in arms." The war thus ruthlessly prosecuted was the prelude to five years of equally atrocious and cruel occupation, in which the robbery, rape and murder of the conquered Ethiopian people by the Italian "master-race" was callously encouraged by the Fascist government in Rome.

Amidst the record of sadistic orgies carried out by the Italian invaders, certain monstrous policies were discerned. There was an effort to thrust a wedge between the Christian and the Moslem peoples of Ethiopia, and to stir up religious and racial enmity between them. Another eyewitness reports in a letter written on the 7th of September, 1936, which was smuggled out of Ethiopia: "The first order given to the Italian armies was to kill everyone carrying the cross. I saw a man pick up a gold cross in the street, and while he had it in his hands an Italian soldier killed him, because he thought he was a Christian. On the following Sunday I saw some Italian soldiers enter an Ethiopian church and ring the bells. Sixteen old men thought it was time for prayer; before they could enter the church the Italians killed them..., I could not help crying, but the Italians were laughing...the dead bodies lay for two days on the steps of the church..."

100

On the 10th of May 1937, six Italian warplanes flew low over the town of Jimma, discharging their bombs unto Ethiopian houses, which were entirely burnt to the ground; hundreds of innocent women and children were burnt to death in the raging inferno thus produced. A policy of extermination was carried out against all the better educated Ethiopians, especially those who had occupied administrative positions. The Italians often invited the chiefs and other prominent citizens to negotiate and then slaughtered them in cold blood.

The terrible massacre in Addis Ababa and other towns on the 19th to the 21st of February 1937, was certainly the worst Fascist barbarity committed during the occupation, although multiple atrocities were constantly perpetrated throughout the entire five years of Italian usurpation.

It was a long established tradition for the Emperor of Ethiopia to make an annual distribution of gifts to the poor and infirm of the city on the 19th of February. The Italian Viceroy, Field Marshal Graziani, decided to ape the Emperor at this ceremony which was held in reverence by all Ethiopians. The Archbishop and other dignitaries not in hiding or exile were ordered to attend. Everything was going well, and the Ethiopians hid their outraged feelings as best they could. Suddenly, hand grenades were hurled towards the table at which Graziani and his lieutenants were sitting. He and the other Italian officers had quickly flung themselves to the ground. The assailant happened to be an Eritrean whom the Italians employed as an interpreter.

A moment of silence followed, which lasted until the Italians realized that no more bombs were to be expected. Then the shooting started as an enraged Italian officer fired with his revolver into the group of Ethiopian dignitaries, while the Italian Carabinieri followed his example. In a few moments there were more than 300 dead in the courtyard and around the palace alone. Hardly a single Ethiopian escaped alive from the courtyard. The general massacre there was particularly senseless and revolting, for the gathered people were mostly aged invalids, blind and crippled beggars and poor mothers of small children. The Italian soldiers ran through the courtyard, seeking any Ethiopians still alive, and shooting any found still breathing.

The grenades had been thrown at 11 am, and a few minutes later, the Italian soldiers and Carabinieri were running all over the city, ordering every shopkeeper to close their doors, and people on the streets were ordered to return home. Within an hour there were no more people in the streets, and postal and telephone communications were suspended. In the palace and neighbouring streets the ground was covered with the dead. What happened afterwards was worse than anyone had anticipated, for the organization of the ensuing massacres was systematic. The corpses of men, women and children, over which vultures would later hover, were lying in all directions, while flames from the burning houses illuminated the African night. The suspension of telegraphic and telephone links in order to prevent people from giving any information to Europe, the closing of the shops and clearing of the streets, were precautionary measures carried out between 11 am and 6 pm.

During that awful night, Ethiopians were thrown into trucks, heavily guarded by armed Italian soldiers. Revolvers, truncheons, rifles and daggers were used to murder unarmed black people of both sexes and all ages. Every black person seen was instantly arrested, bundled into a truck and killed, sometimes at the very moment they were held. Ethiopian homes were searched and then burnt with the people inside, as the Italians used great quantities of benzene and oil to feed the flames. The shooting did not stop for the whole night, but most of the murders were committed with daggers and truncheons. Whole streets were burned down, and if any of the occupants of the houses ran out from the flames, they were machine-gunned or stabbed with shouts of Duce! Duce! while Italian officers passed by in their luxurious cars through the blood-drenched streets accompanied by their wives whom they brought along to view the brutal scenes.

It was a veritable mass murder of the Ethiopian population, and also an immense slaughter of animals as even the animals were not spared from rifles and machine-guns. In the morning the horror continued as homeless people wandered desperately through the streets, seeking their lost relatives. There were dead bodies under and over the Makonnen bridge, and the horror of the bloody sight of thousands of dead, was further exacerbated by the knowledge that these were not combatants fighting with weapon against weapon, but defenceless civilians being murdered.

While the lorries were collecting the dead bodies from the streets, and the blood was congealing upon the ground, Italian soldiers were already rushing to the Bank of Italy branch to change the *thalers* they had stolen in the night from Ethiopian homes, and the gold and silver jewels from the necks of Ethiopian women whom they had murdered. The massacre was so systematic, that three places in the capital city Addis Ababa were appointed for the collection of corpses. Fascists in groups of four or five, heavily armed, again and again attacked single unarmed Ethiopians. No means of destroying human life was neglected, as a second night of massacre followed.

The killing was done in the night to prevent photographs being taken. If any white person ventured into the streets, he was stopped at every corner and searched to see if he had a camera on him. The houses of white people were visited by Italian soldiers, who confiscated cameras. On that second night the military aviation was ordered to bomb the surroundings of the city.

During this time of extreme tribulation, Ethiopia had lost almost ten percent of her population and untold wealth. In 1946 the Ethiopian government presented to the Paris Conference a memorandum reporting the following losses:

Killed in action 275,000

Patriots killed in battle 78,500

Women, children and infirm persons
killed by bombing 17,800

Massacre of February, 1937 30,000

Patriots killed by court martial 24,000

Persons of both sexes who died in
concentration camps 35,000

Persons who died from privations
due to the destruction of their villages 300,000

Total 760,300

Other losses suffered included the burning of 2,000 churches and religious establishments, the destruction of 525,000 homes, the slaughter or confiscation of 5,000,000 beef cattle, 7,000,000 sheep and goats, 1,000,000 horses and mules and 700,000 camels.

Among the numerous atrocities and barbaric acts committed by Italian soldiers during their brutal occupation of Ethiopia, the foregoing stand as an indictment of Italy's savage racial and hegemonic policies under Mussolini s fascist rule: The mass murder of over 600 peasants in Nakamte, the systematic torture of prisoners and burning at the stake of those who refuse to submit to the Italians. The rounding up of thousands of Ethiopian women to concentration camps to serve as prostitutes for Italian soldiers.

During the Italian occupation virtually all schools in Ethiopia were closed down and education for the Ethiopian people was in effect terminated. School buildings were used as barracks for the quartering of Italian troops. In the horrendous massacre of February 1937, when 30,000 lives were sacrificed in Addis Ababa and in other towns, by deliberate policy, the educated youth and all persons who had held directive positions in the country were marked down for slaughter. Of the young graduates and students trained before the invasion, 75 percent were murdered during the Italian occupation. They were the hopeful vanguard of the band of young intellectuals whom the Emperor had prepared by great effort and sacrifice to be the administrators and technicians of modern Ethiopia.

It is of course impossible to describe the demoralizing effect upon the Ethiopian people, of being hunted down and destroyed,

104

day after day, year after year; of having the entire countryside sprayed from the air with poison gas, of witnessing the destruction of churches, the cruel obliteration of human values and especially her Christian civilization which Ethiopia had preserved for over fifteen centuries, and the deprivation of liberty and independence which she had maintained for an even longer period. Such were the extreme conditions with which Ethiopia and her people were faced during this time of her excruciating travail.

Throughout the five years of fascist Roman occupation, numerous Ethiopian patriots joined the resistance groups that continually harassed the enemy forces with constant acts of sabotage, and a stern guerrilla warfare in both urban and rural areas, and which proved to be a source of increasing concern to the enemy. And, although the Italian invaders controlled the capital Addis Ababa and several other towns, many parts of Ethiopia were never subjugated. At the same time, while enduring the rigours of a bitter exile in Britain, His Imperial Majesty Haile Selassie I managed to maintain contact with the resistance forces at home, and was kept informed of the extreme suffering of his people under the savage and barbarous usurpation of Mussolini's fascist hordes.

From the city of Bath in the county of Avon, Haile Selassie and members of the Imperial family, along with a few of his trusted assistants and advisors, continued to receive frequent reports of the situation in Ethiopia, and with the support of British intelligence, coordinated the growing resistance to the Italian invaders. Much of the United Kingdom government administration was removed from London to Bath in World War II. Later on, with the advent of the Great War, Haile Selassie secured British help in forming an army of Ethiopian exiles in the Sudan, which launched a heroic liberation campaign in early 1941. In January of that year, British and Ethiopian forces invaded Ethiopia and several months after captured Addis Ababa, bringing about the collapse of the short-lived Italian East African Empire.

Shortly after, Haile Selassie returned to Ethiopia through Sudan, while the Crown Prince Asfa Wossen entered Ethiopia from South Africa. This separate journey was made to ensure the safety of the Ethiopian Crown; in case one of them died in action, the other will succeed to lead the nation.

Haile Selassie arrived in the capital Addis Ababa to a hero's welcome by his liberated people and was immediately reinstated as Emperor. There was no celebration, however; and as he sadly viewed the devastation and utter destruction wreaked by the unprovoked Italian invasion, He realized the vast magnitude of the task of healing and reconstruction that lay before him and the Ethiopian people.

The King then spoke to his people, and said: "When Italy began to wage a war of aggression against Ethiopia, we knew we were not so well armed as she was, yet we fought with what strength we could muster, because it was our duty to resist an enemy that had come to seize our country. But it was obvious that she was bent on exterminating our people with the unlawful use of poison gas, and so we went to appeal to the League of Nations and claim justice for Ethiopia."

"While in spirit I was constantly with my countrymen, whose blood was pointlessly and ruthlessly shed at the hands of the Italians, many of you were forced to take refuge in foreign lands, others suffered and were being afflicted in the wilderness, in the caves, and in the forests of your own native land."

"How many young men and women, priests and monks were pitilessly massacred by the Italians during these years? The blood and bones of those who were killed with spades and pickaxes, of those whose bodies were split asunder with axes and hammered to death, pierced with bayonets and daggers, clubbed and stoned; and those who were burned alive in their homes with their little children, or who perished of hunger or thirst in prison, have all been crying out for justice."

"Everybody knows that these acts of barbarism and cruelty were not committed in Addis Ababa alone, but also in the provinces of Ethiopia. There is hardly anyone who has not been caught and beaten, kicked, humiliated and imprisoned."

"Five years ago on this very day the fascist forces entered, our capital city, and Mussolini announced to the world that he had established a Roman Empire in our country, Ethiopia. He believed that the land he declared conquered would, forever be in his hands. But you were able to destroy the enemy who were superior to you in numbers and equipment."

"From the Sudan, I entered through central Gojjam where our enemy had strong fortified positions, powerful troops, airplanes and artillery. We found that we had one soldier for every 20 of his. The fact that I was found in the midst of my warriors at once attracted many thousands of men, and, so, I mustered my soldiers who were scattered in every direction in pursuit of the enemy, and I have been able to arrive here at the head of my soldiers."

"I am deeply thankful to Almighty God that I stand today in your midst in my palace, from which the fascist invaders have fled. Today is a day in which Ethiopia is stretching her hands to God in joy and thanksgiving, and revealing her happiness to her children."

He, who was the living legend and repository of the sacred Davidic royal bloodline, and earthly manifestation of the kingly character of the Most High, chose not to glory in the ignominious defeat of the brutal enemy that had ravished his land and its people, but rather, emphatically refused to allow any form of retaliation against Italian prisoners of war, who were fairly treated and duly repatriated to Italy. His Imperial Majesty had consistently displayed in all of his private and public decisions and actions, a magnanimity and greatness of spirit, that were recognized as part of his unique personality. And, at the end of that dark episode, in the long and turbulent history of Ethiopia, it must be concluded that...*THE LION OF THE TRIBE OF JUDAH, HATH PREVAILED!*

The Holy Ark of the Covenant, of which Emperor Haile Selassie was its Divinely appointed custodian, was the most coveted treasure that Mussolini and his Papal mentor eagerly wanted to obtain, and was probably, the principal object of the rapacious Roman attack against Ethiopia. It, however, eluded them, as the sacred Ark remained securely in hiding somewhere at an undisclosed location in one of the many islands in remote Lake Tana, where a single, specially selected Levitical priest, continually ministered to it with the ancient rituals of sacrificial blood and incense.

In 1965, prior to the official visit which Queen Elizabeth II and the Duke of Edinburgh paid to Ethiopia, Emperor Haile Selassie had the Holy Ark removed to the underground sanctuary next to the Church of Saint Mary of Zion in the ancient city of Axum, where the Ark rests in seclusion, to this day.

The complete and self-sacrificing dedication of His Imperial Majesty to the welfare of Ethiopia and his consuming passion for the people, are well known. Even at the advanced age of seventy-six years, he still continued working for up to twenty hours a day, with three hours for sleep and one hour for prayer. It was due to his total commitment to the cause of African liberation and unity, that he came to be regarded as the 'Father of African Unity', and he pioneered, and made Addis Ababa the major centre for the Organization of African Unity.

During the visit that Kwame Nkrumah, first President of Ghana, made to Addis Ababa in 1963, the pet lions which the Emperor usually kept at his side, roared at Nkrumah as he attempted to approach the monarch. His Imperial Majesty instantly stomped his feet firmly on the ground and ordered the huge felines to be quiet, much to the relief of the visiting President and gathered guests. For, as in the days of King Solomon, who also kept lions at the side of his throne, the creatures roared when they sensed the malice and ill-will in the Ghanaian visitor, whose true purpose was not really to pay homage and respect to the founder of the OAU, but rather to be seen as the obvious leader of African liberation and pretender to the office of Chairman of the Organization.

And, as is well known, the Solomonic King rules under the sign of the heraldic Lion of the tribe of Judah, symbolizing that He is the *"Leontomorphic Creator"*, fulfilling also the transmogrified divinity as the Lion becomes Man. It is this ancient mystical heritage that gave Emperor Haile Selassie his famous and celebrated dominion over the fiercest lions.

When in September 1974, a gradual coup by communist elements in the military started eroding the Imperial authority, Haile Selassie accepted with equanimity and philosophical resignation the changing winds of history and the distinctive prophetic destiny that were assigned to him at the beginning, and which *must be fulfilled...*

Not many realized the intense anguish and personal pain that the Emperor underwent when he saw his beloved country, Ethiopia, once a model of stability, maturity and growth as the head and jewel of the crown of Africa, descend into chaos, irrationality and corruption. Ethiopia came to be regarded as the pariah of the world community during the seventeen year long terror of the *Derg* regime, who turned the nation into one of the satellites of the then Marxist Soviet Union.

While heavily guarded in military detention, the enigmatic and aged Emperor still exuded the kingly dignity and poise for which he was so well known, and insisted on being allowed to pray for one hour everyday in the confines of his minuscule private chapel. It was on one of these occasions, around mid-August of 1975, on the third day precisely, after he was allowed to enter the cell-like windowless chapel while the guards remained outside..., that he never came back out...nor was he ever to be found anywhere.

His physical disappearance from out of the very hands of his captors had plunged the criminal regime of Colonel Mengistu Haile Mariam into a veritable crisis, as it could not be explained how this seemingly impossible occurrence took place. Mengistu's first expediency was to have the small contingent that was responsible for guarding the Emperor, transported to a remote military base where they were swiftly executed, and the incident was blanketed by an almost complete secrecy, while the usurper figured out what had really taken place.

Eventually the ruling *Derg* decided to announce to the world that the deposed Emperor Haile Selassie I, had died of natural causes while in military detention, and also, that his body was interred at an undisclosed secret location. Thereafter, an elaborate set of circumstantial events were orchestrated to support the 'official' version, such as the preparation of several – up to six – burial graves, including one on the grounds of the Jubilee palace itself.

Nevertheless, reports from credible sources emanating from Ethiopia, disclose that even up to 1986, some eleven years after the alleged demise of the Emperor, periodic military curfews and extensive search of large urban and rural areas were still taking place, ostensibly in quest of the 'deceased' king, about whom sporadic intelligence claimed, was 'seen' at various locations.

It has been over two decades since that announcement was made by the now deposed Mengistu regime, and, although several sets of human remains have been produced purporting to be those of the Emperor, none have been found to correspond to him. And, whereas the phenomena of bodily translation belongs to the era of Biblical and mystical happenings of a supernatural kind, the possibility that this may have taken place with a person so uniquely marked by divine providence and by manifest destiny, cannot be entirely ruled out.

The sacred Davidic bloodlines continue to be manifested in the persons of the Imperial Princes, the grandsons and great-grandsons of the Illustrious Lion of the Tribe of Judah, all of whom are still living in exile along with other members of the Imperial family. The Crown Council of Ethiopia, a historic advisory body to Ethiopian Monarchs, functioning as the official custodian of the Ethiopian Crown, is also in exile. Yet, although there is a clear line of uninterrupted succession to the throne, those who recognize in Haile Selassie I the fulfillment of the Messianic Biblical promises, assert that no other king will be anointed and crowned in Ethiopia, for He is the Alpha and the Omega, the First and the Last, the immutable seal of the Dynasty of the Blessed Seed.

CHAPTER 5

"Thief on the Cross"

In those days when the kingdom of the Jews was no longer independent under their own native rulers, the Asmonean princes, Jerusalem remained under the rule of Herod and of members of his family; but, was in effect under Rome, till the time of the destruction of the holy city in A.D. 70, when the city was then laid in ruins.

The Hebrews had their own rulers in most of the cities in Palestine, and were allowed to have the same status as the Romans, and the special privileges they demanded as God's chosen people. Having the status of Romans entitled them to a civilian government of their own, independent of the rule of the tribunals in the cities in which they lived. They enjoyed rather unlimited religious liberties, yet they denied those religious privileges to the natives in their own lands who were not of their faith.

In the synagogues where the ruling class of the Hebrews met, the separation of classes and sexes was strictly observed, and women were generally considered as unprepared for administrative positions in the Temple. This attitude towards women is reflected in many passages in the Jewish liturgy used in the synagogues, where thanksgiving is expressed, thus: "Blessed art thou, Lord and God, that thou has not made me a woman." Women were considered as having no souls, and no degree of spirituality that could be developed, and were therefore incapable of becoming angelic. Even in the iconography and statues, angels are always depicted as being males. No rabbi or scribe would permit himself to enter into a religious discussion with a woman, nor would he deal with a woman in respect of spiritual matters.

The Jews silently resented the fact that the scepter of power had been taken away from Judea, and that the chosen people of God were subjected to the government of Rome. This was a humiliation which the Jews hoped to see undone. Israel yearned for, and faithfully hoped that the day would come when her people would rise again in power, and when their 'King of Glory' would appear and reestablish the power and kingdom of Israel again, as in the days of old. And so, Israel waited with suppressed emotion, for the long-awaited coming of that great day.

The House of David, out of which the true leader of the people of Israel should come, had long since passed into the hands of strangers. The high priesthood was Jewish only by their religious profession, as they were politically Roman, and culturally Greek. Therefore the Great Deliverer who would lead them out of bondage as Moses had done, could not come through the lineage of those who were at present at the head of the nation, neither could he come through those who were in the priesthood.

At that time, there was a proliferation of the mystic sects and sacred cults of the Orient throughout the whole land of Palestine, and one of the devout followers of the sacred rituals was one Joachim who was High Priest in the Holy Temple of Helios, or Temple of the Sun, at the outer gates of Jerusalem. He was an adept of the higher orders of the Essene Brotherhood and had pledged his whole life and resources to the great work that was his special calling in life. When the time came that his wife Hannah was to have a child, they agreed that if it should be a girl, and she should show *in her infancy* that she was Divinely ordained, she should become a *dove* in the Holy Temple and remain a Virgin of the Sacred Sanctum.

In the ninth month Hannah bore a child, and it was a girl, just as the Magi (astrologers) of the Temple had predicted. When the days of her purification were accomplished, Hannah gave the child the breast, and called her name Mary, because at the time of her birth, the sun was in the sign of Libra.

When the child was six months old, she was taken by her parents to the Temple so that she might be examined, and that which she carried from her last life be revealed in the presence of the priests and the Magi. The child was placed in the Sanctum upon her own feet, with her face towards the east, while her mother sat upon a white cloth at the foot of the Vestal Fire. The baby was urged to walk and she did walk. The Priests and Magi noticed that the child took *seven steps* and then knelt upon her knees before her mother in the Sanctum. And as the Magi chanted, the mother lifted up her child and cried aloud to the heavens: "As the Lord my God liveth, thou shalt not walk upon this earth until I give thee to the Temple of the Lord." And the priests rejoiced in the fulfillment of the prophecy that Joachim, their High Priest, should give to the Temple a virgin.

The mother, true to her promise, made a sanctuary in her home and placed a cloth from the Temple of Helios upon the floor on which the child Mary should walk, so that she set not foot upon the earth until the day of her deliverance to the Temple. During the time of her upbringing, Hannah suffered nothing common or unclean to pass by her child, and called upon the undefiled Virgins of the Priests of the Temples, to lead her about the improvised sanctuary, and to carry her in arms into the rose gardens when the sun was setting.

And when the child's first birthday came, Joachim brought the child Mary from the sanctuary to the Priests, and she was sprinkled with undefiled water, and the petals of roses, and the Magi proclaimed her officially named Mary, the Dove of Helios. And the Priests blessed her and prayed to God saying: "Oh God of our hearts, bless this child and make her name, as the Magi has just proclaimed it to be, a name to be eternally called in all generations of the sons of God."

When the child attained three years of age and was exceedingly bright with utmost inner understanding, Joachim called the Priests and Scribes of the Twelve Kingdoms and invited the undefiled Virgins of the Priests to escort Mary to the Temple. The virgins came with their sacred lamps burning with joy at the gift of God to the Temple, but the child Mary refused escort and was carried only by her mother to the gate of the Temple, that her feet might not touch the earth.

The virgins were inside the Temple chanting and incensing the Sanctum when Mary was received at the outer portal by the Priests of Helios. The child was then taken into the Temple and placed on the third step leading to the altar while the Sacred Fire burned and the priests chanted and prayed to God, saying: "God hath magnified His purposes and His name in all generations, and through this child God will manifest His redemption to the children of this land."

And they blessed the child, and marveled that she danced with joy and walked by herself from the altar into the Sanctum and knelt before the *Shekinah*. As the parents made their way towards the door of the Temple, they turned and saw that the child asked not to go with them. The parents were surprised at the child's desire to remain alone in the great Temple. When they had departed and the child Mary was alone, she saw her own child body floating as a Dove in the air, and from out of the space above the *Shekinah* there appeared a hand as that of an angel, giving Mary as she floated in the air, a morsel of food, while a voice, seemingly from the angel said: " Behold, this is to be thy food henceforth, for no longer shalt thou find milk at thy mother's breast, for thou hast sucked that which God hath provided, and now thou shalt eat only that which thy spiritual kin shall serve thee."

When Mary attained to the age of twelve years she flowered as a woman, with functions which gave sign and symbol that her day had come when she would fulfill the vow of her parents. So, a council of the Priests and Magi was held, and they said: Behold, Mary the Dove is become twelve years old and she giveth sign that her day either to dwell within the Temple or be given in marriage has come. Shall we take her now, or wait the allotted time of twelve years and eleven months?" And the Magi replied: "Go before the Altar and ask God to show that which is right, and whatever God shall manifest to thee, that will we do."

And Joachim the High Priest entered the Sanctum and placed upon his ritual garments the triangular breastplate, and prayed for illumination. Shortly thereafter a form appeared to him, saying: "Joachim, Joachim, go forth and summon the widowers of the Brotherhood who hath homes, and let them take a sacred staff each, and Mary shall be given to be cared for to him to whom God shall show a sign." And Joachim reported that which was said unto him, and the scribes were informed to bring forth the widowers of their Kingdoms.

Amongst them there was one, by name Joseph, who was of the Essene community at Galilee, and who was a devout brother of the Temple of his Kingdom; and when he heard that all the widowers were summoned to Helios, he laid down his axe and tools with which he was building a house, and hastened to meet the others. When all the widowers were assembled before the Temple of Helios, the High Priest selected 144 sacred staffs and purified them before the altar and gave each of the widowers a staff. Joseph was the last to receive a staff, and as he lifted it in sacred salutation to the High Priest, behold a white dove went out of the rod and hovered over the head of Joseph.

And the High Priest then said to Joseph: "Thou hast been allotted to receive the virgin which hath been given to Helios, to keep with thyself in thy home. But Joseph refused, saying that he knew not what was intended by the gathering of the widowers, and that he had two sons, and furthermore he was old and the virgin appeared to be a young girl not yet thirteen years of age as the law required.

The High Priest admonished Joseph, reminding him what God did to Dathan and Abiram and Korah, how the earth opened up and they were swallowed because of their unbelief. Therefore Joseph feared, and offered to take the virgin and to keep with himself the Dove of Helios. And he said to Mary: "Behold, I have received thee from the Temple of God, and I will leave thee in my house and go to finish that house which I am building, and will then come to thee. And thus came Mary to live with Joseph, the widower and builder.

Some time after Joseph had departed, and Mary was in the house alone, there appeared to her the figure of a great Master who said: "Fear not! I come to bring thee a message of great joy, Mary, Holy Virgin and Sacred Dove of Helios, for thy day hath come to fulfill the prophecy of the Magi! Thou hast found favour with God and thy brethren, and now thou shalt conceive from the word of God." And when Mary heard this she was amazed, and said: "Shall I conceive from the word of God? And yet shall I bear a child as every woman beareth?"

And the voice of the figure said: "Not in the manner of thy understanding shalt thou conceive, but in the manner of thy understanding shalt thou bear. The seed of man shall be thy heritage, but the word of God shall be breathed upon thee, and its power shall make thee holy and bless the seed that it may be of God. And that Holy life which shall be born of thee shall be called the Son of God, and he shall attain the name Iyesus because he shall be the God in Man and will become the God with men." Then Mary answered and said: " It shall be according to the word of God!"

Mary went away to her cousin Elizabeth, and stayed there until her condition was so manifest that she again sought the privacy of her home. When her sixth month came and Joseph returned from his house building and found that Mary was with child, he was surprised and became sorrowful. He smote his face and threw himself upon the sackcloth of the home sanctuary and wept bitterly, saying: "With what face shall I go before my God? For I have received a virgin, and the Dove of our Temple, and have not guarded over her, and thus she has been defiled by man? Who hath done this thing in my home? Is not the history of Adam repeated in me?"

And Joseph arose from his sackcloth and called Mary and said unto her: "Why hast thou who walked the seven steps and was raised to the third step of the Holy of Holies in our Temple, permitted man to defile thee? Didst thou not receive food from the hands of an angel as a token that thou wast not to accept from the profane that which would feed thy earthly desires?" And she wept bitterly also that Joseph should mistrust her, and she cried: "I am pure and know no man!" But Joseph was filled with awe and challenged her words, saying: "Whence then is it that thou art with child? She responded innocently unto him: "As our God liveth I know not how this came about but through the word! As I slept he came unto me with pureness of spirit, freed from the mortal body, and whereas he breathed not the breath of lust but spake with the breath of the word of God, I conceived in fact as God first conceived in thought."

Joseph was afraid lest those who knew not of the laws of God would misunderstand and misjudge. Therefore he was in a quandary. But in the night there came unto him the voice of the Master, saying: "Be not afraid, for that which she hath conceived is of the Holy Spirit, and she shall bear a son and the heavenly hosts shall call his name Iyesus because the Holy Spirit through the word of God, shall be in him."

And the High Priest sent for Joseph and Mary and gave them hearing and listened carefully to Mary's declaration of innocence and purity. The Magi was consulted and it was decided that the test should be given whereby their auras would manifest the colour of sin, if sin there be upon them. Each was given a drink from the vessel containing the radiant water and they were placed in the dark, but only pureness of Light came from them, and no sin was made manifest. And the High Priest said: "If the God of our Temple manifests not thy sin through His laws, then I cannot judge you." So he dismissed them as pure in heart and clean in body.

Some time afterwards, Joseph found it necessary to journey with Mary to avoid censure because of his predicament and Mary's strange experience, and they came to a cave where they rested at Mary's request, for she believed that her hour of travail was at hand. Joseph sought aid and met a woman who came to the cave and met Mary and heard the strange story and believed it not; yet Joseph felt instinctively that at that moment the presence of God was upon the face of the earth, and that some miracle was about to be wrought. While he and the woman waited in the cave, a great Light came into the darkness of the cave and it repelled them, and went and hovered over Mary. And the Light became smaller in size and more dense in brightness until it enveloped Mary and then slowly reduced and disappeared.

Then, as Joseph and the woman watched in silent awe and wonder, there came the cry of a baby and an angel appeared and said unto them: "At this hour, in humility of spirit, and with pureness of mind, to a Virgin of the Temple, there is now born the Son of God, and his name will become Iyesus (Jesus), for that is the name of God into which the fire of spirit and the power of the word is given. But I warn thee not to tell to the profane that which has happened, for they will believe thee not, but will say that unto a Virgin some mortal man hath given child; and they will curse thee as a defiler of thy trust."

Joseph and Mary made ready to depart from the cave where they had been for sometime, and were met by the Magi who came, saying: "Where is the great King whose star in the heavens declares his birth? This hour should see him and his parents upon the road, for the hour of his birth is passed." And Joseph answered and said: "I come into Judea with the Son of God, not the King, for his Kingdom is not of the world but of the hearts of men.

And when King Herod heard that a great King was born who fulfilled the predictions of the prophets, he made inquiries and was troubled. And when the Magi of the Brotherhood heard what Herod threatened, they warned Joseph, while blessing Mary and giving to her their tribute for the Holy man-child; gold because He is a King, frankincense because He is a God, and myrrh because He is a man. And Joseph and Mary proceeded on their way by another road, and fled Judea with the young child and went into the land of Egypt, sojourning there for many months before traveling further south into the dominions of the King of Ethiopia, where they remained for three years and six months.

For there, in that land 'where the Gods love to be', they found refuge and much needed solace and rest. In that remote mountain

Kingdom, the arrival of the Messiah was an event eagerly expected, and their sages and their wise men, and the monks and the nobles and their kings also, diligently observed the signs foretold by the prophets of old, and knew that the day of His coming had arrived. Thus it was that their own King Bazin (or Belshazzar) had journeyed to the birthplace of the Christ, to pay homage and render tribute to the newly born Promised One. King Bazin had reigned in Ethiopia for seventeen years; eight years before the birth of Christ, and nine years after the birth of Christ.

And in that blessed land of Ethiopia, as in most Oriental countries, it is well known that Iyesus was not the first great Master, *Avatar*, or Son of God, to be "born of a virgin", although the authorized Christian version of the virgin birth of Iyesus, presents the story as though it were unique and exclusively a Christian manifestation. To the mystics of the Orient of all ages, the great mystery of the Virgin and spiritual birth of a Son of God is accepted not only as a possibility but as a fact that is natural to the life of every great *Avatar,* for there can be no question that He was divinely conceived and born if He was a Divine Messenger, anointed with unusual authority from on high.

India had a number of *Avatars* or Divine Messengers who were incarnated through Divine conception, and two of them bore the name of "Chrishna", who was born of a chaste virgin called Devaki, who, on account of her purity, was selected to become the mother of God, thereafter being impregnated by Divine sunbeams. When the first Jesuit missionaries visited China, they wrote in their reports that they were appalled at finding in the heathen religion of that country a story of a redeeming master who had been born of a virgin and who was Divinely Conceived. This God, Lao-Tsze, said to have been born 3468 years B.C. of a virgin, was said to have been black in complexion, and described as marvelous and as beautiful as Jasper. Horus was known to all the ancient Egyptians as having been born of the virgin Isis, and his conception and birth was considered one of the three great mysteries or mystical doctrines of the Egyptian religion.

We also find that here in the New World, the tribes of North and South America had Gods that were supposed to have been Divinely born. So, the mystics and enlightened ones throughout the ages, understood that the Saviour and Redeemer, Iyesus, was not the first and only, but the last and greatest of all the messengers of God conceived in this manner and born on earth.

While Joseph and Mary with their blessed child were in the land of Ethiopia, they had received news from Palestine, that the crazed and demented King Herod I had ordered an horrendous and fearful massacre of the newborn male infants in Judea, for thus he expected to thwart the prophesied coming of the King of the Jews, whom he saw as a threat to his rulership. But shortly after, they also learnt that the murderous king had died, and they were told to return to the land of Israel, to the community of Essenes in Galilee, for it was now safe for them to do so.

So they prepared to depart from the country of Ethiopia where they had found a welcome sanctuary from the evil designs of Herod against the Holy child, and slowly they began their journey unto Egypt, going forth with the provisions and the mules that had been given unto them, and they eventually reached the arid and parched territory of Gaza, as they gradually moved on in their exhausting journey through the desert road.

They had made frequent stops on the way, tarrying but only briefly each time, to allow Mary and the young child some repose, and also for Joseph's sake as he was a very old man but yet sturdy for his years.

After resting for a few hours at a small oasis they had encountered on the way, where a few herders of camels had been watering their animals, they rose up and mounted their beasts as the morning sun began to cast long shadows upon the surrounding sand dunes. After traveling but a short distance from the oasis, two bandits suddenly came forth and challenged them, saying: "Whence are you coming from, and where are you going to?" And Joseph answered them saying: "We are travelers journeying forth from the land of Egypt, and we are going towards Palestine."

And these two young bandits whose aspect was fearsome, began callously stripping the old man Joseph of his garments, and began taking of their provisions too, and they stripped the holy child of his garments also, but they troubled not Mary who stood by silently weeping and praying. And as they were about to depart, leaving the traveling family destitute of their provisions, and Joseph and the little child naked of their garments, one of the marauders whose name was Heman, said unto the other one whom he called Mahol: "Wait. Let us return the garments to the old man and the little boy, for I feel sorry for the child who is looking at me with eyes full of sadness." To which the other thief whose name was Mahol, responded: "I will not return to them what we have taken, for these are costly garments which will fetch us a good price at the marketplace. Let us depart hence, for I will not return these garments."

But that thief whose name was Heman, persisted in his desire to give back the stolen goods to the sorrowful family, saying: " We have stolen much during these past days, so then, you can have my part of the loot that we have previously taken, just let us return these unto them, for I cannot bear to see the little boy looking at me in such pity and pain." To which the other bandit, Mahol, then said: "I shall take your part of the loot that we have stored up from before, so you may return to the old man and to the child their things." And Heman, quickly went and returned all that they had taken unto Joseph and the young child, also their provisions, and they hurriedly went away, quickly disappearing behind one of the many sand dunes nearby.

And Joseph and Mary gave thanks unto the Almighty that they were delivered from the hands of the evil one, but they also ascribed blessings unto the Most High for softening the heart of the merciful thief who returned the stolen garments and the provisions to them. And they slowly travelled on and reached the shores of the Sea of Galilee, from whence three brethren of the Essene community met them and accompanied them on the last part of their journey.

The fact that Iyesus was born in the family of two devout

Essenes, was in itself sufficient to guarantee that the young child would acquire the highest education available in any land at that time, due not only to the excellent masters and teachers that were at work in their own preparatory schools, but also to the associations and connections which the Essenes maintained with their own branches in foreign lands.

The Nazarenes, the Nazarites and the Essenes maintained a great monastery and mystery school on Mount Carmel, a venerable and ancient centre for the mystery teachings dating from the times of the prophet Elijah, of whom it is also well known, was a Nazarite and an Essene. At the monastery in Carmel where a "school of the prophets" functioned also, many of the most ancient manuscripts were translated and illuminated on parchment and sent to the various archives of the organization throughout the world.

Around four hundred years after the days of Kristos (Christ), the monastery and school at Mount Carmel were abandoned as the principal place of education for the Essene Brotherhood, and the extensive library with its thousands of manuscripts and ancient records were transferred to the secret monastery of Tibet where they were preserved, and where the greatest school of mysticism and sacred literature in the world was maintained.

According to the ancient records of the Essene Brotherhood, in the sixth year of His life the young Iyesus was placed in the school at Carmel, and there began his preparation and training as a Son of God and as the preordained *Avatar* of the new cycle. He was thus given every special educational advantage that the entire organization in Palestine and in Egypt as well, could give to one that was known to be their special charge and the greatest among them. The authenticity of the above statement has been confirmed by the appearance of several ancient records verifying this fact which was subsequently confirmed by many later incidents in His life.

Virtually no information appears in the Christian Gospels about the life of the Master Iyesus between the time of His examination by the learned doctors in Jerusalem, and the beginning of His mission in Palestine. The first revelation regarding the preparation of the Messiah for His work as a Son of God, is in connection with His baptism at the river Jordan. We are told in the Gospel narratives that at this time Iyesus came out of Galilee and permitted Himself to be known to the public.

But, most certainly, the baptism of Iyesus could not have been the beginning of His preparation for the ministry, as definitely, more preparation than this was required to carry on the work of salvation which He efficiently conducted for many years. And indeed, His whole life demonstrated that He was trained and meticulously honed for His earthly ministry, by deep study, careful preparation, and unusual guidance during His youth.

And according to the Essene records, the young Iyesus completed His official schooling in the School of the Prophets at Carmel, early in the fall, when He was still in His thirteenth year. The instructions that had been sent to the school at Carmel from the Supreme Temple at Heliopolis, instructed that the young *Avatar* was to complete His education by a thorough study of the ancient religions and teachings of the various sects and creeds that were most influential in the development of civilization. He was also to become familiar with the principal teachings of the so-called heathen religions, of pagan beliefs and rites, as well as the higher principles and creeds taught in the mystery schools of Egypt.

And so, the young Iyesus was placed under the guidance of two Magi who came to Carmel for the purpose of conducting the youth to His first distant school and place of experience. They proceeded with a number of others in a caravan to *Jagannath,* on the eastern coast of India, and which is known today as *Puri.* It took them almost one year for the caravan to reach this place in India which had been the center for Buddhism, and where there was a monastery or school containing a large collection of the ancient Buddhist writings. According to the records, the young Iyesus remained for about one year in this monastery school, becoming thoroughly familiar with the ancient teachings and the evolved rituals of the Buddhist faith. From there they proceeded onto Benares and the valley of the Ganges river. In Benares, Iyesus had an opportunity to pursue the study of natural law, ethics, and languages.

Due to his contacts with eminent teachers and learned men in Benares, the young Iyesus was visited by a high priest from Lahore, who tried to persuade Him to change his teachings slightly and also to cease His journeys among the lower castes and the common people. This was Iyesus' first temptation to hold Himself aloof and distant from the common touch and to change His attitude so as to appeal to the aristocracy and the influential. He however, refused to agree to the suggestions of the high priest. It was while He was journeying through these far eastern lands, that Iyesus received news of the death of His father Joseph in Galilee.

While He was still in India, a messenger came to Iyesus with several manuscripts from a Buddhist temple in Lassa, Tibet, that were sent to Him by Meng-tse, considered to be the greatest of all the Buddhist sages. Later on, Iyesus journeyed to Lassa where He remained for almost eighteen months, and from there He went to Persepolis in Persia where arrangements had been made from before, for Him to further His studies there. This was one of the celebrated ancient cities of the kings, and the center of the learned Magi of Persia, one of whom had visited the infant at the time of His birth, and had brought Him gifts from the monastery of Persia.

After spending a year in Persia, Iyesus and His guides went on to the Euphrates region, where He contacted the greatest sages of Assyria, and Magi from other lands who came to see Him and hear Him speak. He spent a considerable time in the cities and towns of Chaldea, and in the lands between the Tigris and Euphrates. They journeyed through the ruins of Babylon, where they viewed the fallen temples, the ruined gates, and the empty palaces. There He became familiar with the trials and tribulations of the early tribe of Judah when they were held in captivity in Babylon, and He saw where Daniel and the Hebrew children had endured their great tests of faith.

Afterwards, they journeyed to Greece, where He came into contact with some of the Athenian philosophers and where He was under the care and personal direction of Apollonius, who opened up the ancient records of all the Grecian lore and traditions for Iyesus. A few months after, He sailed for Alexandria where He remained but for a short time, before He was taken to the city of Heliopolis, where He was approached by representatives of the pagan priesthood of Egypt, who had heard of His teachings and His demonstrations of mystical powers and disapproved of them.

When Iyesus was ready to be admitted into the supreme college and monastery of the Brotherhood at Heliopolis, He was given many of the rarest manuscripts containing the texts of ancient doctrines and creeds, and was subsequently required to enter into a three month-long period of meditation, prayer and study in quiet surroundings. Having completed the three preliminary degrees of initiation, which were really degrees of tests and trials, He was admitted into the Fourth Degree of the Brotherhood and finally honoured with the title of *Master* by the conclave of High Priests, who acknowledged Him as the Christ, and paid homage to Him and proclaimed Him the incarnation of the Word, or *"the Living Logos"*.

By the next day, messengers went forth from Egypt to every land in which branches of the Essene Brotherhood were located, to proclaim the coming of the Saviour and the announcement of His mission of redemption. And so, all the peoples who were ready for the coming of the Lord were duly notified, and the great work of *Iyesus Kristos* (Jesus the Christ) began.

At about that same time in Palestine, there emerged one out of the sturdy race of Judah proclaiming a message which most of the Jews had hoped to hear in their lifetimes, the coming of the Messiah. He came from the wilderness into their midst in pious clothing, and they looked upon him as an ascetic. His camel's hair raiment was a symbol of penitence, and his words were those of an ancient prophet. His special territory was in the valley of the Jordan known as the Sea of Solitude; and the people called

126

him John the Baptizer. And the people came from all parts of Palestine to hear the message of the Baptizer, and to witness his strange ceremonies in the waters of the river. And word came also from other lands, that other prophets were foretelling the coming of the Messiah, as over and over they repeated the ancient prophecy that *"out of the land of Egypt would come the Son of God"*.

The large number of people who gathered in that part of the Jordan - many of them remaining for weeks in the temporary camps that were built- were earnestly hoping that the Messiah would appear in the midst of the thousands who thronged there on feast days. A number of the more militant ones asked permission to form a group to take up the work of John the Baptizer, and to serve under him in the beginning of a *holy war*.

When rumours of this plan reached the rulers of Palestine and the priests at Jerusalem, they began to feel uneasy at the excitement of the populace. At the same time, other conditions in Palestine seemed to indicate that a great crisis was at hand. Tiberius Ceasar, who was now seventy-four years of age, spent most of his time indulging in the most disgusting debauchery and degenerate orgies at Capri, rapidly hastening his demise, while his procurator in Judea, Pontius Pilate, was continuing his persecution of the Jews and becoming more furious and unpredictable.

It was in the midst of these conditions that Iyesus Kristos quietly and without recognition returned to Galilee and greeted His mother, brothers and sisters, shortly after which reports reached Him of the work being done by the Baptizer. Iyesus decided then that He should set the great example among the Gentiles of Galilee, and proceeded to the Jordan to submit Himself to John's Baptism.

The Messiah stepped forth and He and the Baptizer faced each other for the first time since they had met in one of the conclaves in Egypt. Instantly John knew that he was in the presence of Kristos, the Christ, and he folded his arms across his chest with the right hand over his heart, and the left hand over his right breast, making the salutation of Brotherhood typical of the Essenes, and Iyesus replied by making a similar sign. Then Iyesus stepped into the water and submitted *voluntarily* to the baptism.

And thus began the official, public ministry of the Son of God, the great work of redemption which He willingly undertook for the sake of humanity, knowing as He did from within the fortress of His Holiness, that He would come to the final close of His career during a public attack upon His teaching and life, culminating in His crucifixion. Thus, He made prophetic reference, a number of times, to the sad close of His life, which He anticipated and for which He was quietly prepared. He also knew that He would not be the first of the *Avatars* who had been crucified, and who had been accused wrongly by the very people for whose sake He had come into the world.

And, as soon as Iyesus had completed forty days of meditation, prayer and self-examination, He learned that John the Baptizer was already cast into prison because of his missionary work; thus the anointed Messiah of God was aware of the fate that awaited Him, but this did not deter Him nor discourage Him, for all these were but tests of his faithfulness.

And as He went about bringing the good news of the coming Kingdom of Heaven, the multitudes of Palestine followed Him and found peace and renewed life in His words; and His popularity was in ascendancy with the downtrodden, the poor and the destitute, and all those who were forlorn and in despair, while the rulers and the priests at Jerusalem pondered with increasing trepidation and envy, on the reasons for the great appeal that the Galilean prophet had upon the people. He spoke to men, women and children about the marvelous power of humility, of sorrow for others, of the inner goodness of the heart, and hunger and thirst after righteousness, as the mystical doctrines and spiritual principles which were the way to the Kingdom of Heaven.

The Jews of the land of Palestine did not consider Iyesus a Jew, but a Gentile, and many of them ridiculed the idea that anyone from Galilee or anyone who was believed to be a Nazarite could do anything that was good. While it is true that He did criticize some of the practices in the synagogue and in the Temple, this in itself did not bring about their antagonism. Neither was He persecuted for establishing a new religious sect in the land, for among the Jews there were various sects already established, such as the Pharisees, Sadducees, Essenes, Nazarites, Kuthites and many others, and none of the founders of these various sects was ever punished by death.

Iyesus may have proclaimed Himself as a Messiah, but then, any member of the House of Judah might have believed this without being killed by the Jews for holding such a belief. Furthermore, the simple claim of being the "Son of God" would hardly have offended them in any way; for every Jew believed that God was his "Father" and referred to himself as the *Child of God*, this being a common conception of the Deity in Israel. Far more important than the claims that He was a Messiah and the Son of God, was the title being bestowed upon Him by the enthusiastic followers who idolized Him, and who openly proclaimed Him *"King of the Jews"*. This was a very serious matter, and became the real reason for His crucifixion.

In those days the Jews were anxious to have a leader, whether he was the true Messiah or not. The restlessness among the Jews in Palestine and their hopes and plans to be freed from the yoke of Rome had cause Rome considerable anxiety in the past. Everywhere the spies of the Roman administration were watching for the possible uprising or signs of rebellion, or even the selection of a leader who might start another war like that of the Maccabbean freedom fighters. So then, the whisperings or even the open professions of the followers of Iyesus proclaiming Him the *"King of the Jews"* was a matter serious enough to be immediately reported to Rome and be given official attention, and the Roman standing army in Israel and the spies maintained by the Romans made it possible for that government to take stringent measures whenever there seemed to be a possible uprising in the land.

According to reports of that period contained in many ancient records, Iyesus was undoubtedly feared by Rome, since His teachings, which tended towards a sort of *holy socialism*, were opposed to those taught as the official doctrines of the Romans, and the tyrannical imperialism of Rome could never harmonize with such teachings as this. Thus, from the Roman point of view, the only offence that could be attributed to Iyesus, was one of a *political* nature. Furthermore, most of the contentions and revolts that became quite popular in Palestine at about this time were purposely attributed to Iyesus and to his followers; and all this further convinced the Roman authorities of the necessity of removing the leader of this new troublesome movement.

Therefore, by the time the Messiah entered Jerusalem for the purpose of carrying out the culminating final phases of His work, a warrant for His arrest was already in the hands of officials in Jerusalem. But, due to the fact that He arrived at the height of the festival period, it was deemed advisable not to interfere with the sacred peacefulness of the Jewish Feast Days. The leader of the *Sanhedrin*, Caiaphas, had anticipated an uprising when the hour for the arrest came, and such an eventuality would have been disastrous, and would have upset the celebrations of the pilgrims, but also, more importantly, would have seriously diminished the very large financial harvest which always resulted when there were so many thousands of pilgrims in Jerusalem.

There are a number of references contained in rare ancient manuscripts, showing that an assassination of Iyesus had actually been planned by some of the mercenaries of both the religious fanatics of Jerusalem and the local Roman authorities. It was decided, however, that such an act would be blamed on the Jews rather than the Romans, because the Romans had every reason and every power to proceed openly and officially in having Iyesus condemned as a political troublemaker, and needed not therefore, resort to assassination. But then, the officials appointed to arrest Iyesus realized that if they attempted to arrest Him in public while He was preaching or performing His miracles, they would have to contend with a mob situation resulting in the use

130

of arms and force, the destruction of life and property, and a state of affairs not desired by either the Roman authorities or the Jewish people.

It was decided, therefore, to arrest Iyesus in private, when He was outside of the city and accompanied by only His inner circle of followers. Someone was needed, however, who could identify Him from among the others, as they were all usually clad in the customary white raiment of the Essenes, and kept their hair and beards long and curly. Judas was willing to fulfill that role in return for the bribe that was offered him. Yet, the Messiah knew beforehand of the treachery of Judas, as He knew also of the coming events that were about to end His career.

He was well aware that the penalty for insurrection under Roman occupation laws was death by crucifixion, and He knew also of the excruciating agony that the crucified ones undergo before the welcome arrival of death ends their torturous suffering. All this He saw before Him; and the images of His impending ordeal at Golgotha appeared in His mind, racing forth to that appointment with His sacrificial destiny, when He saw Himself upon the Roman cross with two other crucified bodies; one at each side.

The Roman soldiers followed Judas' directions and found Iyesus with a few of His followers in the Garden of Gethsemane, where He usually held secret consultations with Nicodemus, Philopoldi, Mathaeli, and Yousef of Arimathea. While the soldiers proceeded to arrest Iyesus, Yousef of Arimathea hurried away to inform others of what had occurred, and to make immediate plans to aid his Master. The Roman Procurator in Palestine, Pontius Pilate, was consulted and he agreed to delay matters until after the Feast days. He was fearful that in this whole affair there could have been some illegality or some sort of procedural underhandedness, and that criticism against him would result, thereby jeopardizing his own position.

The warrant called for an immediate trial, but Pilate found legal reasons to delay matters without antagonizing the higher

Roman authorities, while at the same time serving his own purposes. There were some who claimed to represent the Jews, and others claiming to be supporters of the Roman government, who called upon Pilate demanding that the order of Ceasar's *prefect* be carried out at once. The warrant was of a nature that called for the death sentence if the person arrested was found guilty as charged. And, although the decisions of the lower judges and witnesses were reported to Pilate that very night, he found not in these decisions that crucial testimony which he believed was sufficient for him to permit immediate execution.

There was an attempt to transfer the case to Galilee, because Iyesus was not a Jew, and therefore bring it under the jurisdiction of Herod, who was attending the Feast in Jerusalem; but this also failed. And Herod himself was not too anxious to take part in an affair that he knew was a more serious matter than appeared on the surface. Meanwhile, the intriguers feared that with such delays Iyesus might slip out of their clutches, but his followers were merely demanding a fair trial and sufficient delay to enable them to prepare their defense of the beloved Master, while the Messiah Himself seemed to be unconcerned regarding the controversy among the higher magistrates, remaining with a peaceful mind, knowing, as He knew, what was really in store for Him.

Finally, Pilate turned Iyesus over to the mob of accusers and personal enemies, and the cruel process of the torturing scourging began as a preliminary to the crucifixion. Meanwhile, the Apostles and the brethren of the Essenes were silently carrying on their plans and appealing to higher authorities to save the life of their Master, while those who knew, realized that Iyesus had advised them of the real nature and purposes of the crucifixion, and of how it would terminate and what in the end it would accomplish for the sake of fallen mankind.

Nearly a week had elapsed since the warrant had been issued, and hour by hour passed until finally the body of Iyesus was raised on the cross on Golgotha, a hill just outside Jerusalem's city walls. Here other condemned men had been crucified, as had been the custom of the Roman occupation authorities for years. The Jews who had gathered round to witness the raising of the cross, dispersed to prepare for the approach of the Sabbath, and only the Gentiles and the brethren of the Essenes remained there to watch and to protect the body of their Master.

And one of the old miscreants who was crucified next to Iyesus insolently reviled him and shouted out, saying: "If thou art Kristos, save yourself and save us too!" And Iyesus recognized the voice as that of the bandit Mahol whom he had encountered as an infant on the desert highway. But the other malefactor rebuked Mahol, saying: "Fear God, for the condemnation is your just reward, yet this man is innocent and free of guilt." Then he said unto Iyesus: "Remember me Lord, when thou comest into thy kingdom." And the Saviour, though benumbed by the wrenching pain coursing through his tortured body, turned his head towards the pleading voice, and instantly recalled the thief known as Heman who had shown mercy unto Him and his parents and had returned their garments and provisions along the desert road so many years before. Then Iyesus said unto him: *"In truth I say unto thee today, Thou shalt be with me in paradise."*

CHAPTER 6

"Divinity on the Slave Ship"

"I will say to the north, Give up; and to the south, keep not back: bring my sons from far, and my daughters from the ends of the earth;"

Isaiah, 43:6

Relentlessly they moved on, away once more from the fertile areas irrigated by the great river, that giver of life that was the sustenance and source of their greatness of old, unto the stretches of the desertic wastes and further south, away from the Mediterranean and the profitable trade routes, leaving behind the eternal monuments in brick and stone that silently testify to a bygone era of remote glory when their seemingly settled permanence gave them an illusory sense of unchanging eternity.

And as Asians and Europeans were entering into the African motherland in increasing numbers, an intensification of the ancient struggle between the invaders and the invaded became inevitable. These were not military invasions, but rather invading settlers who came in a manner that did not at first cause immediate alarm, as it was a gradual infiltration that, over time, brought unbearable pressures to bear upon the local black population. These were the ones who prepared the way and made it easy for the invading armies that came from Asia and Europe.

And this had been going on for countless generations of their ancestry. It was a pattern so long established, that they were now immured to the obvious ravages wrought by disease, malnutrition, wars and the harsh oppression of the Asiatic and European invaders. For even as far back as in the days when recorded history was not, the Africans had taken their first firm stand in Egypt, making a determined heroic effort to hold onto the southern reaches of the land, and even to reverse the unending pressures of the gradual foreign encroachment.

They fought back in a long series of wars to regain their ancient homeland along the Mediterranean, even as they were being subjugated or pushed southwards. And as the third millennium B.C. opened, victory after victory of the Africans over the Asian invaders seemed to indicate that they were regaining their land from the clutches of the usurpers. Thus began the historic First Dynasty when the African King Menes defeated the Asians decisively, and united all Egypt under African rule again. His was one of the longest reigns in ancient history. King Menes instituted profound reforms and innovative changes in the administration of the kingdom, bringing about a stability that laid the foundations for the flowering of African genius in the realms of science, arts, religion, architecture and building, mathematics, medicine, and the crafts.

For those earliest invaders entered the African continent and settled around the Mediterranean, thereby maintaining contact with Europe and Asia, while in the east, northeast and south, they settled along the Red Sea and the Indian Ocean, thereby keeping in touch with their homeland and with the trade with countries farther away. It was thus that Black Africa was hemmed in and effectively cut off from the rest of the world. And this coveted land of the blacks was truly a vast domain, a world to itself covering over 12,000,000 square miles, with its archetypical Ethiopian Empire extending from the Mediterranean north, to the source of the Nile in Abyssinia. In those days Egypt was the northeastern region of ancient Ethiopia, and was the object of world attention from the earliest times, principally because it was in the cen-

135

ter of the crossroads from all directions leading into Africa from Asia and Europe.

The great agricultural system that was developed along the overflowing Nile river was one of the sources of the wealth that gave support to the great cultural advances of the nation. The other was the gold mines below the First Cataract, which was like a magnet that drew the Caucasian peoples from many lands, thereby undermining the bases of Black power. The Blacks had to choose whether to remain in their homeland and be reduced to the status of servants and slaves, or they could migrate southwards as the majority did, and always for the same reason; to escape white oppression.

And these early blacks were themselves a great people, living in settled societies of scientists, architects, engineers, mathematicians, scribes, scholars, organized religions with hierarchies of priesthoods, standing armies and generals, carpenters, brick and stone masons, sculptors, farmers, teachers, slaves, gold and silversmiths, and blacksmiths. But their memorial endured and showed that they were outstanding builders, whose work goes back seemingly into the stone ages.

For Africa had been recognized in antiquity as the "Cradle of Civilization", developers of the oldest written languages, and the blacks were indeed the first Egyptians and the builders of that ancient civilization, long before the bastardizing of the race, brought about by the Asian and some Blacks who, in their eagerness to appease the invaders, freely gave their daughters and other desirable females as gifts to become concubines to the new ruling Asiatic classes. And so it was, that throughout the whole ancient world, the Assyrians, Hebrews, Greeks and Romans, knew of nothing more remote in history than the Black man's civilization.

But in Lower Egypt the steady transformation of the population from black to brown and to white, brought about the division of the former empire, and the characterization of the Egyptian as non-African. So that when Mentuhotep II, the great Elev-

136

enth Dynasty King, reversed the policy of integration with the Asian population and attempted to expel them from lower Egypt and the Delta in 2040 B.C., he quickly found that they could not be expelled *in toto,* for all Lower Egypt was by then overwhelmingly an Asian population from centuries before. Yet, even after the Asian occupation of the Nile delta, the Ethiopian empire still included most of Egypt, along with its lesser divisions of Wawat, Nubia, and Cush.

And in the world of ancient Black Africa, religion occupied the most prominent place. The pervading belief in immortality, in life after death, was accepted as a fact of life and beyond the realm of debate, and was therefore, the great source of inspiration for building such vast monuments in stone and brick, structures that would resist the ravages of time and man, to stand forever. The amazing pyramids and the most elaborate system of temple building that the world has ever known, were done on such massive scale and with such consummate mathematical skill, that today the world stands in awe before these ageless witnesses to the first and greatest civilization ever.

Thebes, the "Mother of Cities" on the banks of the Nile, was the chief center of religion in Africa. Known as the 'University City', the African name for Thebes (Nowe) is the name of the imperial scepter of Ethiopia, a golden staff ribboned with ostrich feathers at the top. So ancient is this "Eternal City of the Blacks" and "City of a Hundred Gates", and its beginning goes so far back in prehistory, that not even a general dating into the stone age can be suggested. With its foundation laid before the dawn of history, its city plan was so magnificent that it was copied by other cities of the world. It was the base for a mighty army from whence 20,000 chariots could be put into the field. Here scholars from foreign lands came to study, and from its learning centers religious ideas and architectural designs spread abroad.

During the Egyptian periods of decline or foreign subjugation, Europe and Asia seized and transported from Africa vast troves of the artifacts of its civilization. From Thebes alone, precious historical material, great treasures in gold and gemstones from the graves and great tombs were steadily plundered over the centuries, denuding the heartland of Black civilization of most of its treasures accumulated over countless generations. The antiquity of this first of all ancient cities may be dimly apprehended, when one considers that many of its formerly great temples were prehistoric ruins even five thousand years ago, and no other city on earth ever had so many temples.

The keepers of the temples of Thebes and other sacred cities elsewhere in the realm, became a powerful priesthood, gradually reducing the power and the influence of kings and rulers, who saw in the mystery of religion a subtle controlling force in the lives of the people, for religion made their subjects submissive and obedient. And as the kings of Egypt became more preoccupied with secular and mundane affairs, the power of the priesthood increased even more.

And through all these millenniums of alternating victories and defeats, trials and tribulations, the elusive dream of uniting the "Two lands" into the former great Ethiopian-Egyptian empire of old, seemed to be an unattainable one, as these Africans battled the invading Asians century after century, extending their resistance against conquest and enslavement to over four thousand years.

And so, the northeastern domain of the former Ethiopian empire, Egypt, continued to withstand the invasions and foreign encroachments of outsiders who accelerated the process of Caucasianization of the Egyptian population. The Jewish rule of Egypt with the Hyksos dynasty lasted 500 years; the Persians 185 years; the Greeks controlled Egypt for 274 years; the Romans for 700 years, and the Arabs for 1,325 years. And this was just the beginning of the long, protracted effort to plunder Africa and its people of all that they had, including their very selves, their souls and even their history and ancestry. Thus it was, that black Africans finally lost all of Egypt, and thereafter, Ethiopia's northernmost boundary began at the First Cataract and its southern reaches were coterminous with present day Ethiopia's borders.

The loss of Egypt adumbrated the further fragmentation of the great Ethiopian empire of old into several smaller kingdoms, and the emergence of the historic transitory kingdoms of Makuria and Alwa after the fall of the great imperial city of Meroe. And while these two African kingdoms were being destroyed by the devastating onslaught of the Arabs, the rebirth of yet another destroyed African nation took place. These were the Funj people who established their capital at Sennar on the Blue Nile, demonstrating that once more another Black fighting state had emerged from the ashes to resist the further Arabization of the African motherland.

The waves of Arab invaders brought with them the threat of an insidious and dehumanizing practice that was destined to have the most profound and destructive consequences for Africa and its people. For, the Arabs' insatiable and perpetual demand for slaves, made slavery and slave-raiding a pervading and cruel institution that instigated and provoked warfare among Africans, expressly for the purpose of enslaving men, women and children for sale and resale. Thus, human beings became profitable merchandise for sale, and the horrendous traffic in human souls began in earnest, spreading to engulf the whole continent, and leaving a sequela that would devastate scores of unborn generations.

And so, the African peoples became the perpetual migrants, an uprooted people who were fugitives in their own land; in movements sometimes slow and gradual, and at other times in tidal waves of forced migrations; but always, from the seventh century A.D. onwards, the waves of Blacks that spread over Africa flowed from the areas where Black concentration was the greatest, and which were the target of relentless attacks by slave raiders and marauding bands of slave merchants. The ancient Ethiopian empire, the "Heartland of the Black Race" was that area of most dense concentration of Blacks.

Countless thousands of anonymous Africans, fleeing from the savage Arab and later European invasions, were migrating from highly civilized centres to less advanced or entirely backward regions where they sank into a state of hopelessness and permanent fear of capture, leading a life in swamps and caves marked by a daily struggle to barely survive, while being constantly on the alert and on retreat from the dreaded slave hunters.

After the year 1,400 A.D. that fleeing mass of humanity, forever moving further and further inland before the mighty firepower of the invaders, became a veritable migratory wave heading either south or west. These people on the run, usually entire families and clans; men, women, children, and the old and infirm too, were not generally aware that they were being slowly hemmed in from all directions. Unaware that while they were aimlessly wandering through the vast stretches of the African hinterland, and that the real danger may be hundreds of miles away, the circle was relentlessly closing in on them, as most of Africa would soon become the world's greatest hunting ground for slaves.

And while the northern and eastern regions of Africa were crumbling under the devastating war machine of the Arab and Asian hordes, across the continent in the west, the three notable empires of Ghana, Mali and Songhay became the temporary sanctuary of part of the fleeing humanity from across the eastern and northern areas of the continent.

Ghana, known as the "Land of Gold", owed its centuries old prosperity not only to its vast resources of the coveted yellow metal, but also to its extensive iron mining and iron manufacturing, as well as the control of caravan trade routes from the east and north and from Egypt and Ethiopia. Eventually, this prosperous West African kingdom succumbed to the slow spreading of the Sahara desert with its ocean of sands swallowing up former green pastures, rivers and lakes. The destruction of its capital Kumbi-Kumbi by the Muslims in 1070 A.D. was another factor that contributed to the demise of Ghana, which saw most of its population fleeing south to the coasts and to the forests.

With the decline of Ghana in the thirteenth century, the kingdom of Mali rose from the epic Battle of Kirina in 1240 to later become the leading empire in West Africa and a major stronghold of the Muslim faith in the region, after their first king

Baranmindanah embraced Islam in 1050 A.D. But because the *Koran* had replaced traditional African laws in the kingdom, intense divisions and rebellions caused deep internal strife and migrations from the country. By the fifteenth to sixteenth century the kingdom of Mali was replaced by the kingdom of Songhai which had its early beginning from as far back as the seventh century A.D. It dominated the gold and ivory caravan commerce of the central regions of the Western Sudan, and became world famous for its renowned centers of learning at Timbuktu, seat of the celebrated University of Sankore, where scholars from many foreign countries and students from all over West Africa congregated.

After some time, the inherent tensions brought about by the enmity between the Black Muslims and the traditionalist African population, erupted in open warfare. All this was further aggravated by the murderous slave traders who had extended their slaving enterprises, headquartered in Zanzibar, far into the interior of central Africa, from whence the slave caravans collected their grim harvest of Black souls for sale to the white slave traders who were fearful to venture far inland. Eventually, these internal conditions in the kingdom of Mali invited attack from outsiders, and the well-armed Muslim forces of the Sultan of Morocco quickly defeated the spear and arrow equipped army of Mali at Tondibi in 1594, signaling the end for the last great West African empire of modern times.

Then began the sweeping invasion of the African continent by Europeans who had been hearing about the enormous land of prosperity, where immense wealth could be had just for the taking. They had been barred for centuries from entering, in spite of numerous attempts and various strategies used. But now, the vast expanse of Africa was there, wide open for conquest and pillage, for the greedy rapine of the 'white devils' with their big ships and their earth-shaking guns, who were about to fulfill the *Great Prophecy* in West African tradition, that *"when the first white man appeared in the land the nation would die."*

The British, the Germans and the French were the first Europeans who started to close in on the continent, and instead of facing the fierce army of defending African warriors, they chose to implement a war of attrition by destroying their great international caravan routes, thereby throwing the country into economic panic and unrest. While this virtual siege began strangling the commercial base of the remaining West African nations, the Europeans were busily building and training strong Black armies that would eagerly decimate their own race and blood brothers at the behest of the white invaders.

And it was between the fifteenth and the seventeenth century that the great encirclement of Africa was accomplished. During this period the Blacks of Africa found themselves hemmed in and threatened from every direction by invading European armies moving forth relentlessly in their march towards world conquest and domination. The technological superiority of the white soldiers was used with devastating efficiency against the bewildered natives, who were being constantly driven into the deep interior regions, pursued by the white hordes of European scum in imperial garb, ruthlessly carrying out the hegemonic lusts of their monarchical patrons.

And these modern European conquerors moved on throughout Africa with a free and unchallenged hand, reordering the Land of the Blacks as they saw fit. Many tribes, clans and family groups had covered such great distances in their flight from the invading enemy, that generations after, at two thousand miles away from their ancestral regions in the Nile valley or Western Sudan or Upper Egypt, they still identified their former homeland.

At one time, the paths they made in their seemingly endless migration could be followed for days by their bloody footprints in the desert sand, and the slave-hunters could determine the various routes of flight by the skeletons found here and there. Those were the ones who wandered aimlessly out into the scorching desert and died with their babies strapped to their backs and larger children clutched by their hands.

Among the many tribes and nations in West Africa during

this period of the European conquest, was the strong confederacy of the Twi-speaking or Akan peoples and who were originally one tribe. They were the Fanti, the Ashanti and the Wassawa; a pastoral race that inhabited the open country beyond the forest belt. They were a single people migrating coastward, part of which, the Ashanti, remained beyond the forest belt on the first terraces of the highlands, while the rest, the Fanti, reached the Gold Coast.

The Ashanti had been a people on the run since many generations before. They and the Bantu tribes descended from Ethiopia, Middle Egypt and Central Sudan, and although it is not known exactly when the Ashanti kingdom was first founded, it appears that after the flight of the Akans from the districts they had formerly occupied and the migration of the Fanti to the coast, the Ashantis remained and settled in the northern portions of the forest country, where they established several minor kingdoms or principalities. By 1640 this confederacy had acquired considerable influence and was regarded as a powerful kingdom. With its allies, it was able to put an army of about 60,000 men in the field.

And somewhere in the remote past, there was an infiltration of the ancient Hebrews in the parent stock from which the Ashanti evolved; this was when the higher classes descended from Eastern Ethiopians were modified by influences from Egypt in the form of Jewish colonists trekking up the Nile, an influence that was eventually to spread itself clear across Africa to the Niger, and from there to the whole of West Africa where it coalesced with an earlier Semitic influence that had swept down from the north.

Gradually, the Ashanti settled down and established a powerful state in Upper Guinea, which for some time embraced nearly the whole Gold Coast also stretching a long way inland. According to their own traditions, the Ashanti are decidedly a race of conquerors; intelligent, industrious and courageous. The loss of much of their earliest history is due mainly to their law which makes the mention of the death of a king a capital offence.

The connection between the Ashanti and the ancient Egyptians and Abyssinians is made patently evident by the striking similarity of most of their laws, customs, religious practices and even extraordinary superstitions. The king of the Ashanti is never to be presumed to speak but through his ministers or interpreters, who invariably repeat even his ordinary observations, preambled with the Ethiopian exhortation: 'Hear what the King says!' The prefix, Zai, in the names of the Ashanti kings is a remnant of the Abyssinian Za which also prefixed the names of the Shepherd kings or original Ethiopians.

Another Ethiopic influence is the part played by the royal women in the succession of the Ashanti kings. This succession is had, not from father to son, but through the sister of the late king to his nephew, as according to the established order of succession in the Ethiopic nation, upon the death of the king, his sister's son ascended the throne, which is also the rule among the Ashanti.

And it is well known that the Abyssinians like the ancient Egyptians, never fight in the night, neither do the Ashanti, not even after sunset, whatever advantages they may lose; and they never fight on a Saturday. And even the custom of stripping to the waist as a sign of respect is found among the Ethiopians and Ashanti alike. Furthermore, the Semitic origin of some of Ashanti customs is demonstrated by the surprising similarity between the supreme being of the Ashanti, *Yame,* and the Hebrew *Yahweh;* and there is a common saying among the Ashanti: "No priest may look upon the face of his God and live," which sounds remarkably like Yahweh's warning to Moses at Mount Sinai: "Thou canst not see my face, for man shall not see me and live." (Exodus 33:20).

One Ashanti proverb is particularly striking; "The Creator created death only for death to kill Him" which resembles either a Christian reference to Calvary, or else a prophetic utterance worthy of Isaiah or some other ancient Hebrew prophet. And there is even to be found among the Ashanti, a remarkable vestige of the Office of the Jewish High Priest in the breastplate worn by their *Osene* (Ambassador) which is strikingly similar to the breastplate of the Hebrew High Priest, even to its division into twelve parts.

And there are many other indications that somewhere in their development as a tribe, the Ashanti came under a strong Hebraic influence, establishing a marked likelihood of intimate historical contact between the parent-stock of the Ashanti and the ancient Hebrews, and the strong probability of Ashanti direct Hebraic descent from the Children of Israel. For this Jewish-Hebrew culture penetrated to West Africa from the north across the desert wastes, and from the east, along the general line of traffic that skirts the great tropical forests, bringing forth the accumulated knowledge and traditions of the largest and most influential group in Africa which has distinctively Jewish descent, the Falashas of Abyssinia.

This steady advance of Hebraic cultural and religious influence up the Nile and westward into the heart of Africa, had truly far-reaching consequences, that were to be seen centuries after in the far lands of the New World of the Americas, where its presence would erupt in surprising and unexpected prophetic manifestations.

And in the times up to the seventh century A.D., Eldad the Danite, an Israelite of the tribe of Dan who had wandered from the eastern regions of Abyssinia to the country of the Cannibals, tells of a Jewish empire known by the name of Aoukar, which long held sway south of the Sahara, having a language seemingly Phoenician and a religion which was that of Joshua, and a Jewish emperor. And this Eldad, son of Mahli the Danite, and who claimed to be a descendant of the tribe of Dan, related that his tribe had migrated from their Palestinian home so as not to take part in the civil war at the time of Jeroboam's secession, and were residing in the land of Havilah beyond the rivers of Ethiopia. Three other tribes, Naphtali, Gad and Asher, were with them; these had joined them in the times of Sennacherib. They had the entire body of Scriptures, and all the laws were cited in the name of Joshua, son of Nun, as he had received them at the hands of Moses.

145

And in those days of Eldad the Danite, the trading and growing commercial power of the Jewish merchants were confirmed by both Arabian and African geographers and historians. These merchants called Rodanites, spoke Hebrew, Persian, Arabic, and the languages of the French, Spaniards and Slavs. From west to east over the whole world, travelling sometimes by land, sometimes by sea, they carried away eunuchs, slaves, women, young boys, beaver-skins, furs and swords, and they brought from China musk, aloes, camphor and cinnamon, entrusting their merchandise to the backs of camels.

They who had been poor and bedraggled peddlers for centuries, now became wealthy and powerful traders. They traveled everywhere, from England to India, from Bohemia to Egypt. Their most common merchandise in those days, beginning with the eighth century, were *slaves*. On every highroad and on every great river and sea, these Jewish traders were to be found with their gangs of shackled prisoners in convoy. And as was the custom of those times, it was considered that the slave-traffickers were actually doing an almost humane and moral duty, for they alone were keeping the conquering armies from slaughtering every one of their defeated foes after each battle.

And those Jewish controlled commercial caravans trod to and fro over the vast expanse of the Saharan sand, beneath which are buried numerous cities and towns, remains of former settlements of the trans-Saharan trade routes. For, in ages gone by this enormous stretch of land was covered by forests, lakes, rivers, orchards, green fields, farms, villages and towns; and wildlife was abundant, and cattle grazed in the meadows. Yet, no prophet came forth to warn the African people that the three million square miles of their fertile land would be made a vast wasteland by the slowly moving sandstorms from the north, that would gradually absorb all waters and desiccate the soil for generations to come.

But the Sahara remains impregnated with biblical legends, from the Ahaggar where the natives claim to have inherited from the prophet Daniel, the secret of finding lost objects by means of magic characters, to the Songhai capital of Koukiya on the Niger river, which furnished the Pharaoh of Egypt with magicians to engage in dispute with Moses, all the way to the Fortunate Islands of the Albion Sea, where the body of Solomon rests 'in a wonderful castle', from whence sprang the sturdy shoot of a hemp tree.

In those days the Ethiopians held the valley of the Nile above Egypt, and all the plateau from which descends the great Nile affluents watering northern Abyssinia with Meroe as its chief town. It was this Meroe that Moses had moved against as general of the Egyptian Pharaoh, before God called him to lead the Children of Israel out of the land of bondage.

When Moses was nourished in the king's palace, he was appointed general of the Egyptian army against the Ethiopians, and he conquered them and married the king's daughter, because, out of affection she delivered the city up to him. Later on, the immense extent of the Sahara was settled by Philistines, and emigrants from Palestine after the death of Goliath. There they mingled with the colony of Israel that had drifted from the Nile Valley, and which established themselves at the southern end of the Sahara. They migrated to the very heart of Africa, unto the banks of the Niger river, where they gradually became absorbed by the Negro tribes and eventually founded what was one of the greatest Black empires of all times, which even after its fall, left its impress on the whole of Western Africa.

On the banks of the Niger are the remains of that original Israelite colony. There the hundreds of wells they had sunk for the irrigation of their gardens can be seen. These wells have been preserved for many centuries; their walls were made of ferroginous stones coated over with the butter of aloes, which the action of a very hot fire had rendered as durable and hard as cast iron.

Timbuktu and the principal oases of the Sahara were known to and visited by Europeans in the Middle Ages, and from the 13th to the 16th century, Europe had established commercial relations with the great centres of the Niger and the Sudan. Dead towns whose past was a glorious one, have left the testimony of their sojourn through history in the numerous remains dotting the southern reaches of the Sahara desert; these are most likely ruins of the old kingdom of Ghana, built by the Jews, those masons of the desert who before the occupation of the Sahara by Islam, reigned there with a Jewish dynasty of at least 44 kings. They were the result of a Jewish migration into the black population of the south, whose language devolved into a form of Hebrew patois, traces of which are still found in the dialects and languages of the Twi-speaking peoples of West Africa, especially among the Ashanti.

Modern scholarship attests to the existence of this Judeo-Negro tribe with a real Jewish element and with a strong Ethiopian-Nubian strain. Its tribal unity was established not on ethnic, but solely on religious lines. Thus, Yame, the Supreme Being of the Ashanti, is the Yahweh of pre-exile Israel in the reign of King Manasseh, typifying the Hebraic culture that found its way long centuries ago, from the Nile valley to the lush regions of the Niger River in West Africa.

As the European nations developed economically and militarily, Black Africans came to be regarded as a cheap and easily obtained labour force for their new colonies in the America's. This was of course fuelled by the numerous accounts of Arab merchants and slavers and of the fantastic wealth of the Kings of Ghana, who prospered by trade in diamonds, gold, ivory and skins. Portuguese slaving expeditions began as early as 1448, claiming from 500 to 700 percent profit on a healthy male slave; and in those early days they could barter with tribal chiefs in the Gambia, obtaining slaves for a few brass rings, leather shields and coloured baskets.

The development of plantations in the New World, signaled the beginning of an enduring economic and political catastrophe for Africa, as the powerful seafaring European nations of England, Spain and The Netherlands, saw the people of Africa as a bountiful source of wealth as slaves.

148

In contemplating the evil and callous exploitation to which Africa and its people were subjected, for a period of four centuries, during which no less than fifty million human beings were captured and transported from one continent to another under the most brutal and systematic enslavement in history, surely qualifies it as the greatest crime against humanity ever perpetrated. The fact that this genocide was conducted under the aegis and direction of Christian monarchies who saw no moral evil in treating men, women and children as so much expendable merchandise, to be used as animals, remains a telling indictment on the whole of Christendom.

Britain and the other criminal monarchies of Western Europe had no intention of bringing a progressive colonization to newly discovered African nations and peoples; but instead, classified those dark-skinned natives as non-humans and unleashed a murderous and undeclared war of attrition, pillage and rapine against Black Africa, from one end of the continent to the other.

Wars between African tribes were deliberately instigated in order to obtain prisoners, and the purchase or capture of slaves became an official policy of the imperial power.

It was the British monarchy in the 1500s that originated the transatlantic slave trade for private profit, as Queen Elizabeth I personally became involved in the despicable commerce of human beings, by pioneering the horrendous enterprise with her own ships, the "Jesus of Lubeck", the "Minion" and, the "Angel". Later on, another slave ship would be grotesquely named the "Grace of God". Thus was inaugurated that barbarous trade that degraded and brutalised all who participated in it.

Elizabethan England in the 16th century was a heartless and inhumane society where death by hanging, drawing and quartering was a common, legal penalty for treason, and prisoners were boiled to death. Even minor crimes such as stealing a loaf of bread, was punishable by frightful mutilations; hand amputations, ear removal, branding, and nose slitting.

The cruel and brutish England under Elizabeth Tudor I, had

nurtured and encouraged the callous greed, the cultural arrogance and notions of racial superiority, which vented its evil passions in the ruthless international exploitation and mass servitude of the black races of Africa.

In the words of the British nobleman Sir William Butler, who arrived in the Gold Coast to take part in the Ashanti Campaign in 1873, "The Gold Coast of Africa has been for over 300 years, the greatest slave preserve in the world. The prison-castles dotting the shoreline at ten-mile intervals, were the holding areas where millions of black Africans were kept, awaiting the arrival of slave ships from Bristol or Liverpool to load the human cargo for West Indian or American ports. A chain of slave skeletons lies at the bottom of the ocean, from the Gold Coast to the West Indian ports. Slaves, Rum and Gunpowder were the chief items in the bills of lading. On the horrendous Middle Passage voyage of that terrible trade, if two in ten of its victims survived, the trade paid a handsome profit."

By 1743 the Treaty of Utrecht established a contract between the King of England and the King of Spain for the supply of 144,000 slaves, by which these monarchs were to *profit personally*, each getting one quarter of the profits.

The number of slaves obtained from Africa at the peak of the slaving commerce was estimated to be over 75,000 a year. Slave hunters penetrated deep into the continent for slaves who would be marched to the ships while being used as beasts of burden, carrying goods weighing up to sixty pounds for at least fifteen miles per day, on journeys lasting up to seventy or eighty days. The time taken to arrive at the coast indicated that slaves were being captured at least one thousand miles inland.

Slaves with their heavy burdens soon became exhausted, but dropping a load was punished by severe whipping. Many who could not continue on the long march, were left on the wayside or were killed by their guards. They were constantly sold and re-sold in different markets so as to confuse them about the route home.

The incredibly horrendous treatment meted out to African captives by the Europeans defied comprehension, and staggered the mind, as the majority of these unfortunate slaves were brought to the West African Gold Coast from hundreds and thousands of miles inland. Most had never even seen the ocean or a ship in their lives.

They were treated barbarously by their masters who beat them mercilessly, whether man, woman or child, subsisting them on the barest minimum in food and drink, with little or no clothing. Their terrible suffering previous to being sold to the slave ship, was a mere foretaste of the living hell they were to undergo in the infamous Middle Passage transatlantic voyage. For many of the captives, the slave ship would become a coffin.

The sheer horror in the minds of the African captives who went through this nightmarish experience can easily be felt, albeit vicariously, when the fact is noted that the slaves readily believed the widespread rumour that the Europeans were buying them to eat their flesh.

All negro slaves were uniformly treated as merchandise, as brutes or animals whose value was measured solely in terms of potential profit and labour for their owner. All their hair was shaved off, so as to disguise their actual age, while their bodies were rubbed with palm oil to give an appearance of sleekness and vitality.

The ship's surgeon had quickly become an expert in selecting strong slaves belonging to tribes which were regarded as a source of good workers. Maximum age for a first-class slave was thirty-five, while older ones and those with defective teeth, eyes or limbs were deemed second-class. The surgeon would keenly look out for venereal sores, as syphilis had already been introduced to Africa by Europeans, and on board ship, would be a source of contamination. Slaves passed as healthy were then branded on the breast with the purchaser's mark.

On most occasions, slave ships anchored off the coast had to wait, sometimes for weeks, in order to purchase or capture their full quota of negroes. On board, all male slaves were shackled in two's, while women and children were battened down in the hold. Any of the slaves who attempted to jump overboard before the ship sailed, had a leg or arm chopped off as a warning to others.

The Middle Passage transatlantic voyage was a truly diabolic means of moving masses of captive Africans to the Americas, punctuated by the cattle-like branding with hot irons on the chest or shoulder, the nauseating stench of large numbers of negroes jammed together in the hold of a slave ship in tropical waters, the pitifully grotesque dances the slaves were forced to perform daily on deck while still chained to each other as a means of exercise, the force-feeding with evil-tasting boiled horse-beans, as the slaves mouths were brutally opened with iron jaw openers.

Restraint was achieved with a double-shackle pinioning the left leg of one slave to the right leg of another. In addition to the shackles, a rope was passed around the necks of every four captives, while at nights the hands were also fettered.

The harsh treatment of Africans on board the slave ships caused an extremely high death rate, especially under the English slavers.

It was indeed common for between two and four hundred deaths from a shipment of six hundred souls to be recorded; but then, even at this dismal rate of attrition, a healthy profit was made. The brutal and heartless attitude that prevailed among the European slavers, was that a percentage of slaves always died, therefore the greater the number carried, the higher the number of eventual sales.

A slave ship on the high seas was easily identified, not only by the stench emanating from it and which sailors in other ships miles away could smell, but also by the sight of sharks following the vessel right across the Atlantic, waiting for the bodies that were daily thrown overboard.

The most frequent cause of death, were the infecto-contagious diseases that were rampant among the human cargo that was stowed in tightly packed rows beneath decks. Lack of ventilation, the foetid body waste and nastiness in the ship's bilge, and malnutrition, inevitably bred the tropical fevers, dysentery, smallpox and virulent infections that decimated the African captives.

Although many deaths among slaves in the Middle Passage voyage to the Caribbean were ascribed to illnesses and disease, such as: consumption, swellings, flux, miscarriage (with subsequent foetal gangrene) numerous others resulted from suicide, self-starvation, jumping overboard from despair and terror, and so on. At times, those who refused to eat had their teeth broken and their mouths opened so that food could be forced down their throats.

The compelling greed and lust for wealth easily obtained, caused many slavers to pack 600 to 700 slaves in a single ship, men having to stand tied to posts, women lying in a narrow space between decks, children crammed in the steerage area while pregnant women were locked together in a cabin.

And, as the British slave entrepreneurs refined and perfected the ruthless efficiency of their robust slave trade, the ports of Bristol and Liverpool prospered mightily and waxed rich from the maritime traffic in human beings, while at Plymouth the local black-smiths were kept busy making hundreds of manacles and leg chains, those opprobrious symbols of bondage.

By 1650 the British occupation of West Indian islands was strengthened by the profitable cultivation of Sugar cane, fueled mainly by the blood, sweat and broken bodies of thousands of African slaves who were relentlessly and brutally worked to death in so many plantation death-camps.

The emergence of a transatlantic "Triangular trade" of British manufactures for Africa, Negro slaves for the insatiable slave markets in the West Indies, and sugar, molasses and rum for England, ensured that large profits were made at each stage of that terrible commerce. Thus was the enormous wealth accumulated by Britannia's criminal exploitation of the African people obtained, a truly gigantic embarrassment of ill-gotten riches which they still hold, and which their descendants enjoy even unto this day.

Chattel slavery and the trade in human beings captured in Africa, created a powerful class of wealthy English families. Financiers in London, directors of shipping firms in Liverpool and Glasgow, merchants in Bristol, steel and iron craftsmen in Sheffield, and many others enjoyed the fruits of their prosperity from slavery, building grandiose palaces and luxurious houses where frequent lavish parties celebrated the massive fortunes of the new idle rich.

By the end of the eighteenth century Britain's international trade, and indeed her whole economy, had become completely dependent on the slave trade. In 1770 the city of Liverpool alone, where the Mayor and every leading citizen was directly involved in the slave trave, boasted of having a fleet of 195 ships engaged in the trade. In that single year that fleet transported over 47,000 Africans to the West Indies.

The magnitude of Britannia's tireless, slaving enterprise in which over fifty million human beings were purchased or captured during the four centuries of Europe's undeclared war against Africa, surely qualifies it as the greatest crime against humanity ever perpetrated. The Nazi-German holocaust of the Jews during the second World War, pales in comparison to the virtual human abattoir that was the transatlantic chattel slavery established by England solely to satisfy her voracious greed and blood-lust. And so, the vaunted British cultural hegemony erected this abominable monument to their great historical condemnation, as in the name of trade and international commerce they shamelessly created the most degrading activity ever conceived by mankind.

As their brutal experience gathered more and more knowledge about the African continent and its people, the European slavers soon realized that not all Africans had the fatalistic temperament which allowed a small number of white men to intimidate and control several hundred slaves during an ocean voyage lasting up to four months. They learned early to identify the slaves coming from recalcitrant, stubborn tribes, who although stronger, were not necessarily good workers, much less obedient and submissive ones.

Thus, the Koromantyn and the priestly aristocracy in their midst, had already gained a fearful reputation as likely troublemakers, both, among the slave traders as well as the planters in the West Indian islands. These remarkable Gold Coast negroes of the Ashanti nation were responsible for a number of mutinies which occurred on board slave ships. These shipborne revolts were serious and disturbing episodes for the slavers, and also for the monarch and the government in London, because plantation buyers offered lower prices for slaves from ships on which rebellion had broken out, since they all knew that once resistance started, it was certain to continue.

The standard policy of a slave's ship crew was to cow and daunt the slaves with merciless brutality. In 1721 the "Elizabeth" which had 500 slaves on board was anchored west of Accra. Three hundred of them were Koromantyns, and even though there were fifty Europeans as crew, they failed to keep the slaves quiet. Soon after, a revolt broke out and three sailors were killed by the rebels.

As the two Koromantyns who led the mutiny were strong and valuable specimens, they were not executed, but rather put in irons and savagely horsewhipped. The other four, among them one woman, being classed as poor specimens, were sentenced to death, two being forced to eat the liver and heart of the third before being hanged and their bodies dismembered and thrown overboard. The woman was hoisted on a yard arm, bestially whipped, and then slashed with knives until she died.

Mutinous slaves who were executed as an example to others, and also to terrify them into submission, were usually laid on deck and their head severed and thrown into the sea. Amputations were most terrifying to Africans, especially to the Gold Coast slaves, whose religious belief holds that an after-life would not be possible if a limb was missing.

And so, among the great numbers and tribal varieties of negro

155

slaves brought from Africa, the fierce Koromantyns occupied a very prominent place, and although their dangerous and rebellious character was well known, their superior strength was so highly valued, that all measures proposed to discourage their importation into Jamaica were totally rejected. Their arrival in this Caribbean island was destined to have dramatic historical significance, as they would leave indelible and unforgettable manifestation of their presence, with a series of daring and heroic deeds in their enduring quest for the freedom they were willing to die for.

Gold Coast Africans were generally known as Koromantyns. Valued by the planters as strong, intelligent and active, they were nevertheless rejected by Spanish and French Colonists on account of their ferocious tendencies. All attempts to legally prevent their importation into Jamaica failed, though they were the instigators and leaders of every slave rebellion in the Island.

The Koromantyns are distinguished from all other negroes by a firmness of body and mind, and a courage and stubbornness which enables them to confront situations of great difficulty and danger, and even to face death in its most horrible shape, with fortitude and indifference. Many of them had undoubtedly been slaves in Africa, and taken captives in battle and sold to the European slave traders. Some were perhaps the owners of slaves themselves, and would thus resort to the most desperate means to regain their lost freedom.

The Koromantyn was pre-eminently an Ashanti who exhibited a fearless independence and an uncompromising spirit, and were distinguished from all other slaves by their courage, resilience and impatience of control. As they maintained a commanding influence over all the other types of slaves, they even imposed on the others their own peculiar superstitions and religious practices.

The evidence of history shows that every slave rebellion in Jamaica originated with, and was generally confined to, the Koromantyns. This fearsome antecedent caused the Legislature of Jamaica to propose a bill for laying an additional importation duty upon the 'Fanti, Akin and Ashanti' negroes, commonly called Koromantyn, that were imported into the island. But, due to their superior physique and strength which rendered them very valuable as labourers, and in spite of their dangerous character, large numbers continued to be introduced to the island.

At the Slave Market auction block held at many Jamaican ports, the female African captives whom by their demeanour or dignified bearing and outward behaviour, reveal a regal background and upbringing, would have their tongue cut out to render them speechless, so that they would be unable to transmit any knowledge of their ancestry, traditions and past glory unto their children and to any of her other tribal kinsfolk.

This most horrendous and cruel mutilation that the British plantocracy inflicted upon the African female royalty, had the long-term, enduring effect of making the mother, and in fact, the black African woman, into a dumb and foolish figure that is despised by her own children and her menfolk.

Even among the children that were brought from the Gold Coast as slaves, manifestations of evident superiority over other African tribes were frequently observed. The Annals of Jamaica[1], relate the incident observed in a plantation where a mixed group of Koromantyn and Ibo boys were to be branded on the breast. The procedure is performed by heating a small silver brand, having the initials of the Planter/Slave-owner, in the flames of spirits of wine, and applying it to the child's skin, which is previously anointed with sweet oil. The application is brief and the pain momentary.

The first one, an Ibo, was brought forward to be branded; he screamed out dreadfully, while the other young Ibos cringed in terror, and the overseer stopped his hand. Immediately, the Koromantyn boys, laughing aloud, came forward of their own accord and offered their bare chests bravely to the red-hot brand.

---

[1] *Annals of Jamaica, G. Bridges, London, 1828*

They each received the flesh-burning impression without flinching in the least, while they scornfully laughed at the tremulous Ibo boys.

Both the Colonial British authorities in Jamaica, as well as the government in London, were shaken by the terrible accounts of the slave rebellion of 1760, which arose at the instigation of a Koromantyn negro, Tacky, who had been a tribal chief in Guinea. The revolt broke out in the parish of Saint Mary in the adjoining estates of "Frontier" and "Trinity", owned by one Zachary Bailey, who had recently acquired over 100 newly imported Gold Coast Africans.

It all happened suddenly, as sometime after midnight, a band of rebel slaves proceeded to the fort at Port Maria where they killed the sentry and took a great quantity of arms and ammunition. After being joined by other slaves from neighbouring plantations, they marched up the main road leading to the interior of the country, leaving death and destruction as they went.

At Ballard's Valley they surrounded the overseer's house at about four in the morning, in which eight or ten white people were in bed, every one of whom they butchered in the most savage manner, and literally drank their blood mixed with rum. At "Esher" and other estates, they also executed a number of white slave masters and then set fire to buildings and cane fields. In one morning they killed over fifty whites, not sparing even infants at the breast, until finally their progress was stopped.

Tacky the chief, was killed in the woods by a pursuing party, while some of the other ringleaders were captured. Gruesome reprisals by the Colonial government followed, so as to make terrible examples of the most guilty.

Of three who were deemed to be involved in the killing at Ballard's valley, one was condemned to be burned alive, and the other two were to be hung up on butcher irons and left to perish in that dreadful position. The slave that was to be burned was made to sit on the ground and his body chained to an iron stake, while the fire was applied to his feet.

He uttered not a groan, and saw his legs reduced to ashes with the utmost firmness and composure. When one of his arms which was tied became loose, he swiftly snatched a burning ember from the fire that was consuming him, and flung it in the face of the executioner. The two that were hung up alive in irons upon the gallows that was erected in the parade in Kingston, never uttered the least complaint, until at length they both died silently on the eight and ninth day.

And this courage or unconcern that the Koromantyn black manifests at the approach of death, arises from their native wars which were savage and sanguinary, during which they demonstrated a cruelty and blood-lust beyond that of any nation that ever existed. There, the captives which are not reserved as slaves, they murder in the most outrageously barbarous manner, cutting them across the face and tearing away the under jaw, which they preserve as a trophy, leaving the miserable victims to perish in that condition.

And also, it was customary in all Ashantiland, that whenever an important man died, several of his wives and a great number of his slaves, were sacrificed at his funeral. This was done that he may be properly attended in the next world.

As to the circumstances leading to the settling of the Koromantyn in the Island of Jamaica, much has been related. While they were excluded from most other slave markets in the West Indies, they were in great demand in Jamaica. Most of them came aboard ships owned by private British slavers who found it necessary to search out and find the best market for their human cargo, and so, they sailed from island to island, where auctioneers and planters in the West Indies would eventually purchase even the weak and not-so-healthy slaves.

These latter were regarded as good bargains because of their low price, and they were worth buying in the expectation that a few months life remained in them,' during which they could be worked to death. But the Koromantyn were prized as a premium buy, as they usually survived beyond the maximum seven years life expectancy of a slave on a plantation in Jamaica.

A West Indian slave market, though it was in those days the grand social and business event in the islands, was emphatically, a vivid illustration of the squalid immorality and national shame to which England had descended in its shocking and degrading treatment of its African slaves.

On the day before the public auction of prime slaves was to be held, they would be fattened-up and made to massage their bodies with oil. Then they would be paraded round the town with much drum beating and flutes playing. Planters were very careful in meticulously selecting new slaves by tribe and language, so that they could be taught by other slaves already in the plantation.

Refuse Negroes who were classed as inferior or second rate, were sold at informal gatherings usually held in the yard of a dockside tavern. These slaves were in very poor shape and often ailing, so buyers had to estimate how much work could be wrung out of them before they died. Smallpox and syphilitic sores and scabs were disguised with a mixture of grease and iron rust, and even slaves suffering from dysentery would have their rectums sealed with wads of hemp oakum used for caulking the seams of ships. Often, these sick and weak slaves were in such bad shape that even bargain hunters ignored them; so they would be left to die where they lay, their bodies later being thrown off the wharf into the sea.

The slave arriving at a plantation in Jamaica would undergo a period of "seasoning", during which the sadistic cruelty and bestial "breaking-in" tortures to promote swift obedience were standard practice. Some of the weakest would inevitably die under the barbarous and often capricious, merciless punishments inflicted by white overseers and chosen black slave-drivers.

Too many instances of extreme torments visited upon hapless slaves in Jamaica are on record in copious historical accounts and archival documentation, which abundantly illustrate the bestial atrocities that were frequent sport and entertainment for planters with sadistic perversions and aberrant tastes.

Ghastly crimes committed against the African slave population were commonplace in Jamaica and throughout the British West Indian islands. The Virgin Islands, Tortola, Nevis, Barbados, and the Leeward Islands, all had their soil soaked with the blood of countless slaves who were murdered with impunity by their masters.

To the white population, the negro slave was an animal. Not to be regarded as a human being. He could be punished in any way the planters, their families and their white employees wished. They would literally work the slaves to death, and freely maim or kill them in cold blood for no reason whatsoever.

There are on record, incidents occurring in remote Jamaican plantations such as one in which twenty slaves forced to work at night, were caught nodding with eyes closed. They were brutally whipped; the number of lashes ranging from 47 to 365, including 291 on a woman. Some of the men were permanently crippled, with one woman dying of her injuries. Neither were children and pregnant women spared. Small children were commonly lowered head first into tubs of water till near drowning, thereafter they were suspended by their wrists and horsewhipped. One ten year old boy was dipped into a cauldron of boiling water.

Real or imagined offences by adult slaves were punished with appalling cruelty. Two Negroes who had annoyed a planter, were pinioned to the ground face down and flogged continuously for more than an hour; both died. In another instance, a privileged slave sent out to locate some runaway slaves, was whipped to death for failing to find them. Another slave, freed from another plantation where he worked as a house slave, was clubbed to death when he grumbled about having to work in the field. Another household slave had a hot iron rammed into his mouth; he later died of his injuries. Two women slaves accused of mixing poison into a planter's food, were held motionless while boiling water was poured down their throats. They died shortly after in frightful agony.

Those who survived the horrors of the Middle Passage and

the subsequent "seasoning period" in the plantation, lived for an average of seven years at most. But for the female African slave, the added burden of intense sexual bondage, frequent rapes and forced prostitution to other planters, or inbreeding by the many studs or 'buck-slaves' kept for such purposes, all became an everyday reality in their stark and hopeless existence. Women slaves were considered primitive animals with strong passions, freely available to quench the basest lusts and, provided all fleshly pleasures demanded by the insatiable white masters. Promiscuity and the wanton breeding of slave women was vigorously encouraged as a means of augmenting the number of slaves on the estate.

It was into these extreme conditions of relentlessly brutal exploitation of the mass of African humanity in the British island of Jamaica, that the Ashanti-Koromantyn Royal Priesthood found themselves immersed, at the end of the seventeenth century.

For they themselves did not escape the long outstretched bloody hand of England's greed and murderous rage against Africa, but also walked through the infamous, narrow "Gate of no Return", from the numerous slave dungeons along the Gold Coast, and unto the slave ships, carried along by the waves of mass deportations from the land of their fathers, towards the new land of bondage… just as in the days of old their far off ancestors toiled in the bitter service of the Egyptians, also for over four hundred years.

****

The Plantocrats in the 17th and 18th century Jamaica were already becoming acquainted with the unease of tyrants who saw their sway coming to an end. They were all aware of the exploits of the feared Maroons, those freed or escaped African slaves who roamed the country and harassed the British forces with constant guerrilla tactics.

The Maroons are principally descendants of the Gold Coast

162

tribes. They claim descendancy from the Ashanti nation, and were active participants in the Jamaica slave rebellion at the end of the 18th century, as partisans of King Cudjoe, their leader.

But the greatest fear of the white slave masters was fanned by their deep-seated dread of the religious practices of the Africans. For, in the drumming, chanting and spirit-possessed dancing, they dimly discerned an atavistic emergence of the ancestral force and indomitable power of the Soul of Africa, which could at any time burst forth in uncontrollable waves of righteous retribution, seeking to avenge the terrible wrong visited upon their ancestors by the cruel and perfidious British.

And so, the British Colonial authorities made every effort to suppress the traditional Jamaica Obeah, which is really a continuation of the Ashanti sorcery of old. As recently as 1908, the "Sub-Officers Guide of Jamaica" by Harry McCrea, Inspector of Police in Kingston, stated that the ancestral practice of Obeah came to Jamaica through the old Ashanti slaves, and was a form of witchcraft wherein its purpose was attained through poison and fear. It stated further that, in "making Obeah", one of the essential elements was a bottle in which various ingredients of the spell or bewitchment were placed.

The implements of Obeah, according to that -official "guide", are: grave dirt, pieces of chalk, small mirrors, beaks, feet or bones of fowl or other birds, teeth of dogs or alligators, human hair, clippings of toe and fingernails, sticks of sulphur, camphor, myhrr, frankincense, packs of cards, and other paraphernalia commonly used in the "black arts".

Even unto this day, these strange practices are well known among the country-folk, who have an abiding fear of, and healthy respect for the power of the Obeah-man or the "Mother" as the female counterpart is known. So it is, that at various places in the Jamaican bush, and most notably in the parishes of Saint Thomas and Saint Mary, during the midnight incantation of Obeah, a collection of these ingredients are placed in a bottle which must be duly buried near the dwelling place of the intended victim.

If the purpose was protective and not vindictive, then, it was openly suspended from a nearby tree or post, being in this case a fetish, pure and simple. The above mentioned "guide" also spoke of the Obeah bottle stuck in the thatch of a hut, or the branches of a plantain tree, to deter thieves.

The darker and more dangerous side of this traditional West African occult practice of Obeah, is that in which poison is used to a fearful extent. The fatal effects of these magic potions are always ascribed to the workings of the spell of Obeah, and never to the actions of scores of poisonous herbs growing wild in every pasture ground, and which are frequently used in the deadly mixture.

After the nocturnal incantation with the preparation of the bottle, the Obeah-man may give his client a powder to be dropped into the food or drink of the intended victim; or, if this is not done, the fact that obeah is being crafted against the individual is gossiped around and quickly comes to the unfortunate's knowledge, with consequent loss of peace of mind. Nervous worry and anxiety would do the rest, and usually the wretched victim would waste away and actually die of fear.

The widespread use of Obeah in Jamaica today is primarily a form of witchcraft as a shield to active poisoning, a claw or tooth, or any other of the usual ingredients of Obeah, may well have been placed in the bottle as a cover for the poison which was to do the real harm. Also, the bottle might be said to be bewitched by the claw or the tooth therein (bottle-witchcraft).

And this pervasive Ashanti influence still persists in the old traditions of the Jamaica bush, with its many "bush remedies" practiced to this day, such as the herbal tea made from certain leaves and twigs known only to the old woman who gathers them, and which effectively breaks a persistent fever; or the throbbing headache quickly relieved by the application of split cactus. Very often the Obeah-man makes use of this knowledge of herbs in connection with his art.

Another powerful expression of the West African tradition

among the descendants of Gold Coast slaves, was seen in the vibrant and irrepressible dancing which forms a very essential part of the Ashanti worship, which has invariably deep religious significance. Here again was seen another strong indication of the Ashanti dominance among the descendants of the slaves in the Island of Jamaica. And the women would rendezvous with ancestral spirits that were invoked by the drumbeat, the mournful chanting and sinuous dancing, as around the flames of the ritual fire they would in wild abandon dance with the spirits.

And although the slave masters did suppress and discourage any manifestation of the traditional religion of their captives, the strong atavistic impulses in the blood of Africa's progeny would burst forth at clandestine gatherings in remote secret caves and hidden ravines, where the drums pulsated ancient rhythms that seemed to wrap the heart.

For, by immersing themselves in the ecstatic drumbeat and the hypnotic fumes of burning seeds and herbs, they were transported in the spirit to the land of their fathers, to their beloved ancestral motherland from whence they were plucked by the savage hand of the 'Despoiler of Nations', Britannia.

And so, the spirit of Judah, rightful custodian of the Scepter of Righteousness remained as in the days of the Babylonian captivity, subdued and dormant, quietly living on through many generations of the Ashanti-Koromantyn aristocracy now laboring bitterly under the lash of slavery in the tropical canefields of Jamaica, nurturing its soul at the deep fountain of its African spirituality and Royal heritage, patiently awaiting the advent of their deliverer... for surely, it had been prophesied that He would emerge as the Lion of the Tribe of Judah from the House of David.

But this Judah was not the Judah of Ezra and Nehemiah, remnant of those who lamented for seventy years of their sojourn in bondage by the rivers of Babylon. The priestly caste of the Koromantyn were the spiritual inheritors of the African Judah that did not go into Babylonian captivity; this was the Judah that in the days of King Solomon, had transmigrated to the land of

Ethiopia, for, when God's Holy Ark of the Covenant had departed from Jerusalem with Solomon's royal son by the Queen of Sheba, Menyelek I, the glory and presence of God had likewise turned aside to go forth and to reside in Ethiopia, the New Zion.[1]

And as the warm breath of Africa fanned human passions into flame, Messianic impulses of liberation mingled with a righteous anger at the tragic and cruel fate that befell their people, spawned heroic slave leaders who conceived and led a number of rebellions against the colonial authorities. Most were speedily crushed and their leaders executed. Others gained support among sectors of the slave population, mainly the Ashanti, and through the instrumentality of the 'talking drums' which were used to effectively rouse into action groups of slaves in distant plantations, they would swiftly turn on their white tormentors with cutlasses, hoes, and whatever they could lay hands on, while other rebel slaves would release a number of mongoose with burning dry grass on its tail in the midst of the canefields. This latter was, understandably, among the most serious acts of sabotage in plantation days Jamaica.

These episodes of insurrection by African captives continued with disturbing frequency throughout the island, while a rising indignation and moral campaign against the inherent evil of slavery gained strength and persuasive force in the forum of world opinion and within England itself also.

Thus, in 1838 came about the epochal legislative act of Emancipation that signaled legal freedom for countless thousands in the West Indies. This however, was not the product of British magnanimity and generosity, but rather the result of a historical moral enlightenment that swept through the consciousness of mankind in the early 19th century, forcing arrogant Britannia to behold the enormity of its genocidal crime against humanity, resulting in that squalid pseudo act of contrition called Emancipation.

---

[1] See Part III African Zion in "KEBRA NAGAST" (The Glory of Kings) LMH Publishing Ltd. & The Red Sea Press.

Yet, less than thirty years after this legal abolition of chattel slavery by England, the wretched conditions of abject exploitation, injustice, discrimination and hopelessness of the newly freed former captives, became intolerable to the point of making rebellion through heroic action, inevitable.

The importation of East Indian indentured workers for the sugar estates, the fall in the price of sugar along with a prolonged drought, further exacerbated an already tense and dangerous social and economic imbalance on the island. Furthermore, the Colonial government refused to protect the people from the depredations of unjust employers and racist magistrates.

And so it was that in October 1865, freed slaves in the rural parish of Saint Thomas led by the indomitable Paul Bogle marched towards the courthouse in Morant Bay where they interrupted a court session, demanding that their voices be heard and their petitions be duly considered. Soldiers were called out and the people set fire to the courthouse. In the ensuing fighting and rioting, eighteen police and soldiers were killed, as well as the Custos of the parish.

Reprisals were swift and overwhelming as the authorities panicked and resorted to wide scale and brutal repression. The government shot and hanged 439 of Bogle's followers, flogged 600 men and women and destroyed over 1,000 houses which belonged to black people. The insurrectionist's leaders, Paul Bogle and George William Gordon were duly hanged.

The Morant Bay rebellion marked the last major rebellion on the island by African slaves descendants, the tremors of which rocked the very foundations of Britain's hegemonic world empire, and marked the beginning of her gradual retreat and the contraction of that great domain over which "the sun never sets".

And for the Ashanti-Koromantyn Royalty, the punishing captivity they underwent in this "Land of Wood and Water" proved to be a purifying experience of mystical renewal, for they perceived and became aware of a providential destiny that had charted their path of bitterness as they went forth from Africa to the Americas, carriers of the truth that cometh from an ancient land, once more to be unveiled and to bear magnificent fruits, when in the fullness of time the majesty and power of the Almighty would be revealed in supreme glory and dignity.

They understood fully that oracular mystery of old, typified in the rivalry between the Northern Kingdom of Israel and the Kingdom of Judah. For when the ten tribes of Israel were taken into captivity by the Assyrians, later to be "lost" and scattered, they emerged under new identities to form new nations, with other cultural characteristics and languages in far and distant lands.

For, as the true Judah, the African Zion in Abyssinia eventually settled in Ashantiland in West Africa, so the degenerate survivals of ancient Semitic-Israelite culture diffused by the Lost Ten Tribes of Israel, ended up in the British Isles, elusive wanderers who rose as a mixed people, mongrel in religion as well as in blood they quickly became assimilated and lost their identity, being absorbed by the people with whom they dwelt.

And as Judah's royal lineage ended with the captivity and death of King Zedekiah and his sons in Babylon, the Almighty ensured that his solemn covenant with David by which He promised that there will always be a descendant of his seed reigning upon his throne, remained true in continuous fulfillment. "The remnant that is escaped of the House of Judah shall again take root downward and bear fruit upward," Isaiah 37:31-32.

So, Judah, having the throne 130 years after Israel had been taken captive, is brought down to the low stature of slavery, and Israel is exalted by continuing the Royal Davidic line in a new land, with their own David-descended kingly line.

Of the twin sons of the patriarch Judah, Pharez and Zarah (Genesis 38:27-30), it was Pharez's descendants who held the throne in Judea, right up to the death of King Zedekiah and his sons in Babylon. Zarah's line never ruled in Israel. But history shows that the descendants of Zarah became wanderers, journeying to the north within the confines of the Scythian nations, their descendants later migrating to Ireland in the days of King David.

Lost Israel under another identity, headed by the tribes of Ephraim and Manasseh as settled in Ireland, seen as a Gentile nation, would flourish and become prosperous in due time, possessing the promised Abrahamic birthright, becoming a colonizing people spreading around the world and being blessed with resources and wealth. At the time of their greatness, powerful and dominant, David's throne will also be found transplanted among them.

"Moreover I will appoint a place for my people Israel, and will plant them, that they may dwell in a place of their own, *and move no more.*" (II Samuel 7:10) That place of their own is the British Isles, the place where the prophet Jeremiah planted David's Israelite throne more than 2,500 years ago, paralleling also the transfer of Judah from Jerusalem to Ethiopia in the days of King Solomon with the taking of the Ark of the Covenant by his son Menyelek I.

The Kings of Judah from David to Zedekiah form eighteen links in the royal chain of succession. The sceptre is then passed down through the daughter of Zedekiah, the Princess Tea Tephi, who was taken to Ireland by the Prophet Jeremiah in 569 B.C. along with Hereman, son of the King of Ireland, who was in Jerusalem at the time of the Babylonian seige of the city. Heremon had married the Princess, and their young son was with them also.

The successors of Princess Tea Tephi and King Heremon of Ireland ruled from 578 B.C. to 487 A.D. forming fifty-five links in the royal chain. Thirteen links of the Royal House of Argylshire passes it on to the Sovereigns of Scotland up to 834 A.D., and the chain is finally completed by the twenty-five Scottish links and the successors of James I of England.

The Ancient Annals of Ireland tell us that when Jeremiah came to Ireland with the royal party, he had with him some remarkable things, including a harp, a replica of the Ark of the Covenant, and a wonderful stone, Jacob's Pillow (Genesis 28:18). Many kings in the history of Ireland, Scotland, and England have been

169

crowned sitting over this stone, including the present queen. The stone rests today in Westminster Abbey in London, and the coronation chair is built over and around it. Jacob's name was changed to Israel by God, (Genesis 32:28). Jacob's Pillow or Pillar-stone is also called "The Stone of Destiny."

And the secret knowledge and heritage so carefully nurtured by the Royal Ashanti-Koromantyn Priesthood and their descendants, gave them great strength and unshakeable faith, for they knew that the cruel captivity they were enduring under British chattel slavery, was the antitype of that typical war between brothers of old, when the Kingdom was rent asunder under Solomon's son Rehoboam, and Judah and Israel made war against each other, until at length they were both taken into captivity, Israel by the Assyrians and Judah by the Babylonians.

They also knew that this African Judah's period of enslavement in the West would end at the appointed time, and that their enforced spiritual night of silence was destined to be sealed by the prophetic force of their divine mission. At that time, from within their midst, there would emerge a powerful voice infused with the Soul of the Bantu, the Soul of Mother Africa, that would announce redemption and salvation for all Africans.

The esoteric religious knowledge carried from Africa unto the lands of the Western Hemisphere by the Koromantyn priesthood, held that the domination of Israel (Britain) over the ancestral African Judah (Ashanti), would be only for an appointed time. Then, "In that day will I raise up the tabernacle of David that is fallen, and close up the breaches thereof... and I will bring again the captivity of my people Israel and they shall build the waste cities and inhabit them, and I will plant them upon their land, and they shall no more be pulled up out of their land which I have given them, saith the Lord thy God" (Amos 9:11-15).

Then, in the decade of the 1930's there emerged among the scattered remnant of the African Diaspora in the West, the powerful proclamations of a millenarian, African triumphalism announcing that the Ethiopian Prince Ras Tafari Makonnen crowned

Haile Selassie I is the living God. It was the great African-Jamaican visionary and prophet Marcus Garvey who had announced that when a king was crowned in Africa, the time of redemption for all Africans was at hand.

When Haile Selassie was crowned in Ethiopia in November, 1930, it was seen by many as a fulfillment of Garvey's prophetic utterance. Thus was born the Rastafarian faith, the first indigenous spiritual-religious movement in Jamaica whose main doctrinal tenets call for a return to the African motherland of her scattered children, and holds that Africa-Ethiopia is the true Zion, the Promised land, and that Haile Selassie is the returned Messiah, the Christ, the Living God, Jah Ras Tafari.

The early pioneers of the Rastafarian movement, among them, Leonard Howell, Nathaniel Hibbert and Archibald Dunkley, had already been proclaiming these ideas which were current in Pan-African circles and among the downtrodden slum dwellers in Kingston, Jamaica. A further resurgence of African pride was strengthened by the 'Back-to-Africa' movement of Garveys popular mass organization, the Universal Negro Improvement Association (UNIA) which grew to become a truly international confraternity of African descendants, seeking to restore racial pride, dignity and self-respect, and to revive the past ancient glory of Africa's greatness.

The historical and Biblical evidence that the Negus Haile Selassie is the Saviour-God who would redeem Israel and gather the remnants of the children of Israel who are scattered among the nations of the earth, is overwhelming. Not only are the titles of the Negus soundly Biblical; King of Kings, Lord of Lords, Conquering Lion of the Tribe of Judah...(Revelation 5:2,5; 19:16; I Timothy 6:15), but Ethiopia herself is Biblically designated as the land chosen by God to be the place of his habitation on earth, (Psalm 68:32; 87:4), as well as being the first nation mentioned in Scriptures, and the seat of the Garden of Eden, (Genesis 2:13).

Throughout the Old Testament, the Messianic promise of a Redeemer who would be the ultimate Liberator and Emancipator

171

of the human race remains a constant central theme. This anointed of Yahweh who would come only out of the Tribe of Judah from the Royal House of David, will be raised up as the Vanquisher of the Enemies of God's people, those wicked rulers of the Babylonian Gentile nations along with their cohorts in apostate Christendom.

Due to the uncompromising prophetic utterances of Rastafarians, their denunciation of injustice and exploitation of the poor by the inheritors of the Colonial masters, and their mere presence and distinctive ethics and lifestyle, as well as their strident anti-Roman and anti-Papal position, their millennarian Messianism would inevitably have a strong political impact that proved to be most disturbing to the establishment. Rastafarian beliefs had a profound impact upon Jamaican culture, an impact and influence that became even more pervasive as the movement grew in strength and acceptance especially among the destitute youth of the inner city.

Although most analysts of the movement saw it as a cultic system of beliefs, born spontaneously out of the frustrations of the embittered, ostracised and forlorn masses of unemployed in the teeming slums of Jamaica's capital city, Kingston, Rastafari is really a rebirth of the ancient Israelite-Ethiopian religion of West Africa with its marked Hebraic influence, and which transmigrated from the Nile valley and the Ethiopian highlands, settling centuries after in the Ashantiland of Ghana and the Gold Coast.

After being refined and tested in the crucible of captivity, and having emerged from under the lash of slavery with renewed power and vision, this progeny of Mother Africa, reincarnated spirits of the heroic Koromantyn Royal priesthood, became the conscience of the nation, resolutely beckoning as Ambassadors of the Most High, Jah Rastafari, unto all of Africa's scattered children, to look towards the ancient Motherland for redemption and eternal fulfillment.

The wider society and the government of Jamaica saw in the

social separatism of Rastafari, a growing threat to the 'status quo' and the established order of things as inherited from the British. The sacramental and ritualistic use of Ganja (Marijuana) by Rastafarians, through which they achieve exalted states of religious experience by an afflatus of the soul and communion with Jah the Almighty, further brought the movement into confrontation with the authorities.

In the early days of the movement's history, the persecution and repression of the brethren was relentless and furiously rabid in its intolerance and desire to stamp out all forms of Rastafari manifestations. In the decade of the 1930s, the commune that they had established at 'Pinnacle' in the Parish of Saint Thomas, was destroyed by government forces and the peaceful settlers were dispersed and forced to abandon the area. Victims of nefarious and pernicious propaganda emanating from sundry establishmentarian sources, the brethren of the Rastafarian faith were further alienated from the mainstream of a society entrapped in a European mindset and lifestyle which caused them to reject anyone or anything that reminded them of their blackness and African origins.

During this early stage of the development of the movement, a number of notable leaders and spiritual guides emerged from their midst who would dramatically impact upon the conscience of the Jamaican nation. Amongst those who left their mark in the contemporary history of Jamaica was 'Cyrus' the Reverend Claudius Henry, 'Repairer of the Breach'.

From as early as 1930 he had traveled to Ethiopia where he was ordained into the Egyptian Ethiopian Zion Coptic Church and had an interview with the Negus. In 1936 after establishing the First Zion Coptic African Reform Church in Jamaica, he was jailed and charged for sedition and blasphemy for preaching the Black Christ in the person of H.I.M. Haile Selassie I. During the decade of the fifties and into 1960, his populist 'Back-to-Africa' movement, with a membership of over 30,000 adherents, had formed itself into a self-sufficient commune based in the Parish of Clarendon.

A series of isolated and far-flung incidents involving other Rastafarians were blamed on Henry's organization, bringing about a protracted campaign of repression and persecution of his followers, which although officially sanctioned by the Colonial British authorities, found in the middle class "browns" and other pretentious new emulators and imitators of the European slave masters, the most vicious persecutors of their own black brothers and sisters.

When 'Cyrus' the Reverend Claudius Henry was brought before the court of justice, he was told by the presiding judge that he was being ordered to "keep the peace", to which Henry asked: "Your Honour, do you mean that I should not preach to my people?" The judge replied, "Oh no Mr. Henry... not at all... you may preach *to your people,* but leave Her Majesty's loyal subjects alone."

Before he was sentenced to prison, the trial judge, Chief Justice Sir Herbert Duffus said to him, "Henry, your doctrine is a *Wicked Lying* one; it is like that of Leonard Howell who came to this country thirty-five years ago with his Rastafarian doctrine and misled the people, and now he is in the lunatic asylum" (Sabbath morning, 29th of October, 1960).

After being released from prison, having served a ten year sentence for treason and felony, Henry issued the following public statement: "I declare, to the Government and the People of Jamaica, that my recent incarceration, not withstanding the humiliation and embarrassment caused, have left me void of animosity, vindictiveness or hatred. It was most unfortunate that my purpose, aims and objectives were wrongly evaluated and misunderstood, resulting in my incarceration. Let it however be understood that my ambition was to be able to continue my work, to establish an organization based on *Peace and Love,* geared to help the less fortunate, regardless of creed, colour or national origin. This, let it be firmly and emphatically known, was to be strictly a Welfare organization which was *non-political and nonviolent.*"

"As you will understand, I am prohibited from being published by the press, radio or television, so, my only medium of public communication therefore, is by means of pamphlets. The government has also confiscated my passport, my religious credentials and preacher's licence, Certificate of Ordination and other documents of a personal nature, and so I am unable to go and do God's work as I am instructed by Him. I, however cherish no hatred in my heart towards anyone."

"Since therefore, the Government is determined that I should not take the message of God's Kingdom to people in other lands, I shall build in Jamaica a New Jerusalem with the cooperation of those Rastafarians who are willing to organize and centralize for the achievement of this objective."

"The Children of Israel and the Children of Judah were oppressed together under white rulers and black oppressors, who took them into captivity and still hold fast unto them. But their Redeemer is mighty and strong, The Lion of the Tribe of Judah, from the Root of David, The Ancient of Days, His Imperial Majesty Haile Selassie I, who has given unto us His Saints, the Rastafarians, His Righteous Judgment to execute, and to build Him a New Jerusalem in Jamaica."

Claudius Henry 'Cyrus', the Repairer of the Breach, went through the Great Transition in 1987 and was posthumously awarded the Centenary Gold Medal of the Battle of Adwa by the Ethiopian Crown Council, in recognition of his long struggle and leadership for Black Pride and Dignity within the Spiritual Movement of Rastafari.

During the decade of the 1970's Claudius Henry was courted and paid homage to, by many political pretenders who were eager for power. They saw in his spiritual Africanist movement a significant populist platform with great potential within the heated political contests of those days. He however, gave his support and that of his organization to the charismatic and persuasive leftist-leader Michael Manley, a skillful and manipulative 'artisan of the spoken word', unto whom Henry had given the 'Rod

175

of Correction' or 'Rod of Joshua', a wooden staff with alleged magical-supernatural powers that had been given to Henry by HIM Haile Selassie.

Although Michael Manley was the son of Claudius Henry's relentless judicial persecutor, Norman Manley, he had nevertheless seen in the younger Manley the requisite qualities of mass leadership, which, with the evident adulation of Jamaica's tens of thousands of suffering Blacks, had made him the 'Champion of the Poor'. With Henry's blessing and with the mysterious powers of the Rod, which Manley duly carried with him in showy exhibition at numerous political gatherings, he went on to win the 1972 national elections and became Prime Minister of Jamaica.

Jamaica's flamboyant new leader, however, quickly succumbed to the seduction of the communist camp's "Third World" rhetoric, and eventually turned his back on the promises he had made to Claudius Henry, that he would champion the "Back to Africa" aspirations of the majority of his people, and especially of the Rastafarians. At length, the international Rastafarian movement, which had gained world prominence with the powerful prophetic utterances of it's "Messengers of JAH", Bob Marley, Peter Tosh, Bunny Wailer, Garnett Silk and many others, was marked for destruction.

The designs and purposes of the enemies of Africa and of her Children, were not circumscribed merely to the obliteration of the worldwide prophetic movement of Rastafari, but because their principal rallying cry of Repatriation (to Africa) was linked to a demand for Reparations (from Britain), the elimination of the Ethiopian Monarchy and its exalted King, the Emperor Haile Selassie, became an obsession for the enemy who feared the resurgence of a powerful and mighty Black Africa.

And when the Negus beheld and realized that the dream of his Children in the West had been betrayed by the one unto whom the Rod had been entrusted, he called unto Cyrus, for the Rod to be returned to Ethiopia. But the Rod was not returned, for he who now possessed it was drunk with power and never did believe in the mystery and mystical force of the staff, and so, the Rod was burnt with fire upon the soil of Jamaica.

And at that very moment began the lamentation for the land, as the prophet had said, "...She had strong rods for the sceptres of them that bore rule, and her stature was exalted... her strong rods ...the fire consumed them... and now she is planted in the wilderness ...and fire is gone out of a rod of her branches...so that she had no strong rod to be a sceptre to rule. This is a lamentation...and shall be for a lamentation. (Ezekiel 19:11-14).

For, Manley had allied himself to the Godless Soviets and their lackeys, Castro and Mengistu, and they made war against the Lamb, and the prophets were slain and the King's crown and the diadem was removed and the Kingdom was overturned, (Ezekiel 21:26-27), that the prophecy be fulfilled... Till Shiloh come.

And the 'crablike pestilence which no man cureth' gnawed at the entrails of the Betrayer, until at length he perished away, a pitied shadow of his former obscene handsomeness; and his memorial shall in like manner be swept away like wind-tossed chaff, to join the forgotten ones who also had trampled on the birthright of their own people, for to deliver them into a new captivity,

But the chosen ones of Judah, the Ashanti-Koromantyn Royal Priesthood and their seed after them...the Children of the NEGUS... the Nation of Rastafari...the Majestic Progeny of Ethiopia, shall continue to abide for many days in this, their 'Land of Sojourn and Increase' until that day when the Messengers of the Most High shall exclaim with them: "Oh that the salvation of Israel were come out of Zion! When God bringeth back the captivity of his people, Jacob shall rejoice, and Israel shall be glad." (Psalm 53:6).

Bibliography and
Recommended Reading

"NEGUS": Ancient Ethiopian title approximating to King; Negusa Negast approximates to Emperor, or King of Kings; the Regent, Ras Tafari Makonnen, was created Negus in 1928, and Emperor (Negusa Negast) in 1930, adopting his baptismal name Haile Selassie (Might of the Trinity) on succeeding to the Imperial Throne.

Henry Barth, *Travels and Discoveries in North and Central Africa*, New York, 1857.

Pedro Paez, *Historia de Etiopia,* Livraria Civilizacao Editora-Porto Lisbon, Portugal, (n.d.)

Rodman R.Clayson, *Egypt's Ancient Heritage*, Supreme Grand Lodge of AMORC, San Jose, Calif. 1971

Harry H. Johnston, *History of the Colonization of Africa by Alien Races,* Cambridge, 1913

Esteves Pereira, *Chronica de Susenyos rey d'Etiopia,* Lisbon, Portugal, 1900

J. Spencer Trimingham, *Islam in Ethiopia*, Oxford, 1952

Harold G. Marcus, *Haile Selassie I: The Formative Years,* Red Sea Press, Trenton, NJ

Harold G.Marcus, *The Life and Times of Menelik II Ethiopia 1844-1913* RSP

Miguel F. Brooks, *Kebra Nagast (The Glory of Kings) The True Ark of the Covenant* LMH Publishers Ltd., Kingston, Jamaica,W.I. / Red Sea Press, Trenton, NJ 1996

George G. M. James, *Stolen Legacy,* Africa World Press, Trenton, NJ 1992

Jean Doresse, *Ethiopia,* Elek Books, London, 1956

Drusilla D. Houston, *Wonderful Ethiopians of the Ancient Cushite Empire*, Black Classics Press, Baltimore, MD 1926

Chancellor Williams, *The Destruction of Black Civilization,* Third World Press, (n.d.)

Rupert Lewis, *Marcus Garvey, Anti-Colonial Champion,* Africa World Press 1988

Ernest Budge, *History of Ethiopia,* London 1928

Ernest Budge, *Legends of Our Lady Mary, The Perpetual Virgin*, London, 1923

Theodore Bent, *The Sacred City of the Ethiopians* (n.d.)

Guebra Selassie, *Chronique du regne de Menelik II, Roi des Rois d'Ethiopie*, Paris 1932, Translated from the Amharic by Tesfa Selassie, (2 Vols.)

Baigent, Leigh and Lincoln, *The Messianic Legacy*, Dell Publishing, New York, 1992

Baigent, Leighand Lincoln, *Holy Blood, Holy Grail*; Dell Publishing, New York, 1990

Sylvia Pankhurst, *Ethiopia, A Cultural History*; Lalibela House, Essex, England

Joseph J. Williams, *Hebrewisms of West Africa*, The Dial Press, New York, 1930

Josephus, *Complete Works*, Translated by William Whiston, Kregel Publications, Grand Rapids, MI 1960

Post Wheeler, *The Golden Legend of Ethiopia*, London,1936

Sellier and Russell, *Ancient Secrets of the Bible*, Dell Publishing, New York, 1994

Joseph J. Harris, *Pillars in Ethiopian History*, Howard University Press, Washington, DC 1981

F. George Kay, *The Shameful Trade*, Frederick Muller, Ltd. London, 1967

Haile Selassie I, *My Life and Ethiopia's Progress,* (The Official Auto-biography of H.I.M.)

Alberto Sbacchi, *Legacy of Bitterness, Ethiopia and Fascist Italy*; Red Sea Press

Dale Bisnauth, *History of Religions in the Caribbean*, Kingston Publishers Ltd. 1989

Richard Pankhurst, *Social History of Ethiopia*, Red Sea Press 1992

Teshale Tibebu, *The Making of Modern Ethiopia: 1896-1974*, Red Sea Press 1995

Chris Prouty, *Empress Taytu and Menelik II, Ethiopia 1883-1910* RSP

Jean Suret-Canale, *Essays on African History*, Africa World Press, Trenton, NJ 1988

Roland B. Dixon, *Racial History of Man*, New York, 1923

George Buchanan Gray, *Sacrifice in the Old Testament*, Oxford, 1925

Andrew Lang, *Magic and Religion*, London, 1901

Wilson D.Wallis, *Messiahs: Christian and Pagan*, Boston, 1918

L. Spencer Lewis, *Mystical Life of Jesus*, Supreme Grand Lodge of AMORC, San Jose, Calif. 1929

Max Schmidt, *Primitive Races of Mankind*, London,1926

Paul Radin, *Monotheism Among Primitive Peoples*, London, 1924

Charles P. Lucas, *Partition and Colonization of Africa*, Oxford, 1922

Kaufmann Kohler, *Jewish Theology*, New York, 1928

W. C. Willoughby, *The Soul of the Bantu*, New York, 1928

John Gladstone, *Facts Relating to Slavery*, London, 1830

E. M.Cook, *Jamaica: The Lodestone of the Caribbean*, Bristol, 1924

Bessie Pullen-Bury, *Ethiopia in Exile*, London, 1905

John Beecham, *Ashantee and the Gold Coast*, London, 1841

Maurice H. Farbridge, *Studies in Biblical and Semitic Symbolism*, London, 1923

Blaise Cendrars, *The African Saga*, New York, 1927

John Roscoe, *The Soul of Central Africa*, London, 1922

Ismar Elbogen, *History of the Jews after the Fall of the Jewish State*, Cincinnati, OH 1926

A.W. F. Blunt, *Israel Before Christ*, London, 1926

David G. Einstein, *The Indestructible Faith*, New York, 1927

T.Eric Peet *Egypt and the Old Testament*, Boston, 1923

Manuel L. Ortega, *Los Hebreos en Marruecos*, Madrid, Spain 1919

Samuel A. B. Mercer, *Ethiopic Liturgy: Its Sources, Development and Present Form*, Milwaukee, WI 1915

Sidney Mendelssohn, *The Jews in Africa*, London, 1920

Brian Brown, *Wisdom of the Hebrews*, New York, 1921

G. Murdock, *Africa: Its People and their Cultural History*, McGraw-Hill, 1959

Karen Armstrong, *Muhammed: A Western Attempt to understand Islam*, Golancz, 1991

Kamal Salibi, *Secrets of the Bible People,* Saqi Books, London, 1988

Archaeology: An Official Publication of the Archaeological Institute of America, Vol. 45 No. 2 March/April 1992 *"Who were the Israelites?"* by Neil Silberman

Theodore Parfitt, *The Thirteenth Gate: Travels among the Lost Tribes of Israel,* Weidenfeld & Nicholson, London, 1987

Edward Ullendorf, *The Ethiopians,* Oxford, 1960

Graham Hanckock, *The Sign and the Seal: A Quest for the Lost Ark of the Covenant,* Heinemann, 1992

David A.Hubbard, *The Literary Sources of the Kebra Nagast,* University of St. Andrews (Scotland) Ph.D. thesis. 1956

Carlo Conti Rossini, *Storia dEtiopia,* Bergamo, Italy 1928

Kamal Salibi, *The Bible came from Arabia*, Saqi Books, London (n.d.)

James B.Pritchard (editor) *Solomon and Sheba,* Phaidon, 1974

D. Kessler, *The Falashas: The Forgotten Jews of Ethiopia,* Shocken, New York, 1985

Biblical Research Committee, General Conference of Seventh Day Adventists, *The Sanctuary and The Atonement (Biblical, Historical, and Theological Studies)* Review and Herald Publishing Assoc. Washington, D.C., 1981

Aldo Lavagnini, *El Secreto Masonico,* Editorial Kier, S.A., Buenos Aires, Argentina, 1980

Gordon M. Hyde (Editor) *Biblical Hermeneutics,* Review and Herald Publishing Asscn., Washington, D.C. 1974

Rex Nettleford, Identity Race and Protest in Jamaica, William Morrow & Co., New York, 1972.

E.S.P. McPherson, Rastafari and Politics, Black International Iyahbinghi Press, Frankfield, Jamaica, W.I. 1991

Cane Hope Felder (Editor) African Heritage Study Bible, James Winston Publishing Co. Nashville, Tenn. 1993.

About the Author

Dr. Miguel F. Brooks is a Historical and Biblical Researcher, Lecturer and Public Speaker, and an activist in the African Holocaust Reparation Movement. Born in Panamá of Jamaican parents, he is a graduate of the Instituto Istmeño in Panamá and Universidad de Carabobo in Venezuela. A member of several academic and philosophic societies, he holds a B.Sc. degree in General Sciences and a Ph.D. in Psychology.

Dr. Brooks was awarded the Centenary Gold Medal of the Battle of Adwa by the Ethiopian Crown Council for his work on behalf of Ethiopian Culture and History. He is the translator/Editor of KEBRA NAGAST (The Glory of Kings) the Sacred Book of Ethipoia.

Printed in the United States
4657